Bristol Radical Pam

Nautical W

Women sailors and the women of sailortowns: A forgotten diaspora c.1693 - 1902

Rosemary L. Caldicott

ISBN 978-1-911522-46-1

Bristol Radical History Group
2019.
www.brh.org.uk~brh@brh.org.uk

Contents

List of Illustrations

Page 54—The Press Gang—Also published under the title 'Hibernian method of raising volunteers'. Artist unknown. Published London, 1770. The names on the banners refer to John Wilkes (1727-1797), radical MP and publisher of *The North Briton*; George Montagu Dunk, 2nd Earl of Halifax (1716-1771); and John Montagu, 4th Earl of Sandwich (1718-1792). Halifax and Sandwich were involved in bringing Wilkes to trial for seditious libel when he accused King George III of lying. See https://www.historytoday.com/richard-cavendish/john-wilkes-expelled-house-commons for more details.

Page 59—The Liberty of the Subject—By James Gillray (1756-1815), William Humphrey: London (publisher), 1779.

Page 94—Fisherwomen, Cullercoats—Winslow Homer (1836-1910), 1881. The original is in Honolulu Museum of Art. For more details of Winslow Homer in Cullercoats, Tyne and Wear, and for many more of his paintings of fisherwomen see https://eclecticlight.co/2016/02/27/winslow-homer-in-cullercoats-3-women-at-work/.

Acknowledgements

I would like to express my thanks to Maureen Ball who kindly assisted me by taking the time to read an almost completed first draft, and also to Mike Richardson who read through my final draft and for his encouraging comments. I am also very grateful to Barbara Segal who undertook a final proofread. My appreciation to Di Parkin for her help in researching the records of early ship stewardesses. I am very grateful to Dr Roger Ball for his support, knowledge and suggestions regarding the history of the Royal African Company. My thanks to my son, Nicholas Caldicott, who assisted me with statistical calculations. Finally, to the in-house editorial team and everyone who has supported me while I pondered the theme, and during the months that I actually got down to writing this work.

Preface

When I started researching cross-dressing women sailors I had visions of women who were fearless, strong and could match a man at work; women who wanted to have fun, travel the world and become financially independent. There certainly is an element of truth to this portrayal. However, the women also tell a sad story of lost love, being abused as a child, or being victims of a cruel economic and repressive system imposed upon women. Although maverick adventurers did exist, and some of them were undoubtedly very successful in their maritime careers, they were nearly always treated as a superfluous curiosity once discovered. Of course the following narratives are only of the women we know about, who when their disguise was uncovered had to explain themselves, often in court. I soon intriguingly discovered the largely forgotten lives of the women living on the margins of our great oceans, residing in 'sailortowns'. Their experiences of life were very different from the women who inhabited rural and suburban spaces because they were always, in one way or another, dependent upon the sea and upon those who sailed the vast oceans. In this work I attempt to tell the accounts of not only the women who sailed upon the high seas disguised as men, but also of the forgotten women living willingly, or unwillingly, on the margins of port life, in sailortowns.

Remove all women and dogs off the ship as we are leaving port.

—Admiral Lord Nelson

ANNE JANE THORNTON,

THE

FEMALE SAILOR.

Introduction

A woman at sea—the crew's misery,
Woman on board—stay at port.

Myths, alongside the sub-culture of women dressing up as men and disguising themselves as sailors, are buried in the historical chronicles of both the British Merchant Navy and British Royal Naval records. Small glimpses of the role of women on board ships are to be found secreted in ships' journals, court records, penned depictions, ballads and artistic portrayals. Much of this story is told in the words of the lost generations of sailors who were exposed as being women, masquerading as male sailors and occasionally even as maritime soldiers. The authenticity of these accounts is made all the more credible by allowing seafaring women in history to recall, in their own words, why they had an attraction to seafaring life and the reasons why they ran away to sea. The autobiographical and analytical approach to the narratives will not only describe female circumstance in an age when women had no legal rights, but also focuses on their lives and validates their stories in the context of the language of the day.

Women have always been linked to the sea and to waterways the world over. But sadly their nautical history has been overlooked in favour of male seafaring pursuits and traditions. As a consequence, as in so many human endeavours, it has become traditional for the male perspective to dominate nautical history. Women were fundamental in supporting and occupying the water's edge space traditionally reserved for women in their support of nautical men in occupations such as dockyard workers and fishermen. But what about the trailblazing women on the margins, for example women who cross-dressed to become sailors? Or the women who engaged in riots and uprisings in support of their seafaring men? Their neglected history will be explored in depth in the work that follows.

Women were also notorious pirates, such as Anne Bonny and Mary Read who were sentenced to death for piracy in 1720, though both women managed to escape the noose. However, women pirates have been extensively written about and will not be examined here. Instead, I intend to concentrate on lesser-known women who sailed the seas; female cabin boys, women who worked on the shoreline, and the women who were exploited.

Another group of nautically connected women were the African women who were forced onto vessels to be sold as slaves, and who sailed alongside the occasional black woman who worked on board slave ships. During the 1740s, 36,700 African slaves were taken to the West Indies exclusively on

The pirates Anne Bonny and Mary Read.

Bristol ships making Bristol the leading slave trade port in the British Isles at this time.[1] Bristol's involvement in the slave trade is only touched upon here, but the extraordinary story of a discovered black women working on the slaver known as the *Hannibal* is recounted as well as the consequences of this odious trade for all that sailed on her.

Part One sets out to contextualise the historical and political background, examining the condition of seafarers during the eighteenth and nineteenth centuries. This section also attempts to offer a framework to emphasise the economic and social environment of the time, which ultimately prompted some women to go to the extreme lengths of disguising themselves as men to have the dissident right to go to sea.

It is also important to consider the women living in large naval and merchant ports as well as those women inhabiting small fishing villages, because all their lives were directly impacted by working conditions at sea. These women were instrumental in supporting male sailors while remaining in the domestic sphere, often taking in hidden work, and working for very low wages while raising large families. Principally these women were allied to a local economy, sustained mainly from the wages of male sailors and the supporting industries on the quayside, such as providing food and provisions for sailors, taking in laundry and perhaps salting fish, for example. As a

---

1   Morgan K. *Bristol and the Atlantic Trade.* Cambridge 1993 p.133. Cited in Pool S. & Rogers N. *Bristol from Below: Law, Authority and Protest in a Georgian City. Studies in Early Modern Cultural, Political and Social History.* p.7. The Boydell Press. 2017.

consequence, they were often embroiled, along with the men, in the struggle to establish their human rights, decent labour conditions and fairer wage structures. These steadfast women sympathised and engaged in resistance movements against poverty, often by being involved in violent revolts, and engaging in assaults against the dreaded and despised press gangs.

Women had restrictions put upon them to limit their means of work, which predominantly meant employment being carried out as 'hidden' work in the home, especially for the middling classes. The trend of home working continued well into the early twentieth century, with women working from the home on very low wages as laundresses, milliners, embroiderers, home bakers and other such enterprises. However, during a time of industrial revolution the new urban working class woman, in the interests of maximum profit, was now to be tolerated as cheap labour in the mines, manufacturing and also in heavy labour dependent factories such as mills. Peter Linebaugh writes that in the past the deprivation of homeworkers' living conditions led to prostitution, large numbers of suicides, starvations and crime, particularly in London and sailortowns.[2]

Women from differing ethnicities who ran away to sea are also referred to, since their stories are equally as remarkable and because they faced the double prejudice of not only being a woman but also on the grounds of not being white. There were many black sailors in the Royal Navy and Merchant Navy in previous centuries. Some were recruited by the British Navy during the American wars in return for being granted a quasi-freedom. There would have been a few black women sailors disguised as men, but sadly most of the stories of black women sailors have been lost apart from a few reports recorded during the American War of Independence. In British ports there would have been a minority of black women and men residing and working, some of whom were inter-married. Disappointingly, their stories are only told in relation to their being a servant for a wealthy white person because at the time to have a black servant/slave was considered a status symbol by the fashionable merchant classes in Britain. Examples of black servants living and working in Bristol can be seen in several paintings. Firstly, in the controversial painting by Richard Jeffreys Lewis, '*The death of Edward Colston*' that includes a kneeling African woman kissing his hand. This woman is believed by many to be 'black Mary', who was a servant named in his will. Secondly, there is a painting by sailor and artist Nicholas Pocock who sketched Sydenham Teast's shipyard in Bristol during 1760. In this sketch there are at least two figures

---

2 Linebaugh P. *The London Hanged. Crime and Civil Society by the Eighteenth Century.* p.143. Verso. 2006. Note: Sailortown is used as a generic word for port cities or towns, either merchant or naval.

of African or Afro-Caribbean men to be seen working in the yard.3 Those often forgotten identities of black women represent an ethnically diverse community who resided in Bristol throughout the early modern era.

During the pre-twentieth century era that this work discusses, strict gender stereotypes were the norm and governed by a conservative patriarchy; by church, civil law, cultural norms and naval law, all of which our women had to circumnavigate. Women had little or no rights and their lives were mapped out for them appropriate to the class they were born into, and the rules for their lives were decreed by men. Eighteenth and nineteenth century predetermined doctrines of assumed gender roles based upon sex at birth meant that if a woman expressed an interest in travel, to sail the seas as a sailor, or simply to embark aboard a ship to be a 'tourist', she might be considered insane, and even in some cases incarcerated into an asylum. For those women who dared to go to sea, they could only get away with acting the male by cross-dressing for a limited amount of time.

In Part Two women tell their own stories and explain why they disguised themselves as men to go to sea. One such discovered woman sailor tells of how she bought herself a quilted waistcoat to hide her shape and a straight wire girdle to disguise her waist in order to live the life of a man. Another woman explains how she would bind her breasts and cut off her hair into a boyish crop to achieve the outward appearance of being male. The advantage of using the women's narratives, recorded in their own words, is that we capture the sense of what life was like for these women and thereby avoid placing present day interpretations onto their choices.

However, for the women who were seeking an alternative lifestyle, for whatever reason, they certainly had to have an adventurous spirit! Dressing up as a man or boy was a way out of drudgery for proletarian women and into a new world of freedom to travel, and even perhaps a pathway to permanent relocation in another country. A sense of adventure could never be suppressed in such women–women of independent spirit and mind. However, the reality for most of these women is that a departure into unknown hierarchical masculine territory, upon the high seas, was in fact prompted by an act of desperation. For example, Mary Anne Arnold was discovered to be a sailor in 1839. Orphaned as a young girl and employed in a rope factory in Sheerness earning 2s 6d (12½p) a week, she noticed boys working on the boats were earning more money and were much better fed than her. Mary Anne used her initiative and borrowed boys clothing in order to sign on as a sailor boy. She worked hard and was given great praise when she was discovered by the

3   Pocock's sketch can be viewed at Bristol's Museum and Art Gallery. Townsend T. *Bristol & Clifton Slave Trade Trails*. p.15 & p.45. PiXZ Books. 2016.

Mary Lacy, who passed a shipwright apprenticeship exam under the name of William Chandler in 1770.

captain—"I have seen Miss Arnold amongst the first aloft to reef the mizzen-top-gallant-sail, during a heavy gale in the Bay of Biscay". Her story tells us that Mary Anne was treated very kindly on the *East Indiaman* after she stopped working as a sailor-boy. She was given her own cabin and looked after by the women passengers for the remainder of the voyage, and apparently she received her pay in full on her return to shore.[4]

Many nautical women were highly skilled crafts-people, such as Mary Lacy who served as a carpenter and shipwright in the navy from 1759 to 1771, in disguise and under the male name of William Chandler. Many women also had proven sailing skills, which were recognised by their male peers after they were discovered. Such a woman was Elizabeth Bowden who, disguised as a boy, joined the British Navy in 1807 under the assumed male name John Bowden. After being discovered, she remained on board sailing with the crew and worked as a cabin attendant. Further examples of naval women sailors are recounted in Part Two.

4 Wojtczak H. *British Women's Emancipation since the Renaissance.* http://www.historyofwomen.org

Due to the restrictions placed upon women in history, it has been necessary to analyse the political, historical and social circumstances of male sailors and women shore workers in some detail, particularly in Part One. This approach will contextualise the difficulties that affected and shaped the women caught up in nautical incidents that took place, both at sea and on the land. At the time the women's accounts were usually recorded as an appendix to the male experience, and therefore only scant records of the lives of the women in sailortowns and on board ship are to be found. The lack of original female narrative is a direct consequence of the fact that men were the recorders of history, whether this was in the form of journals, newspaper reporting, admiralty records, government documents, mariners' fiction, or the officers' records on board ship.

In a male dominated world, and the consequential subordination of women, it was inevitable that the story of the woman would be overlooked unless there was an exceptionally unique or notorious woman involved. To overcome this limitation it has been possible to carefully chronicle and bring to life certain events in history that are usually found hidden in the sub-text. By piecing together the scant details scattered throughout various versions of events, and other academic research already undertaken, I have collected together the stories of some extraordinary early nautical women, told where possible in their own words, bringing together the fascinating accounts of the female maritime world.

Throughout this work women are referred to in the adult female purely for the purposes of literary ease, but by using the term 'women' this will mean, in some instances, the text is referring to girls. Where the evidence allows, I have sourced examples of nautical women from Bristol and the South West of England. However, to widen the political context of maritime proletarian history, paradigms have been included from further afield to include: sailors' working and living conditions, resistance to press gangs, cruel punishments, slave ships, wage disputes, and denied shore leave, to name just a few of the hardships experienced by nautical women. Doubtless our nautical women would have witnessed and been subjected to many unpleasant seafaring experiences, but very little is recorded about their reactions to witnessed events. Despite this, I have attempted to piece together the limited evidence that has survived.

The themes that run throughout this work are all interlinked. The men and women who sailed upon the high seas were interconnected in the maritime struggle to obtain better wages and working conditions for every sailor and dockyard worker during an era of world-wide uprisings, mutiny and revolutionary influences. The lives of women who suffered much hardship under an unfair patriarchal political system, and the forgotten history of the women living in sailortowns, completely dependent on maritime commerce and a naval driven economy, are explored in the following pages.

Knowledgeable of the ways of ships and the reality of life as a sailor, the sailortown inhabitants would have been only too aware that they were about to be left alone to their on-shore life when the Blue Peter flag was hoisted at the masthead of a ship about to sail. The signal meant 'All persons report on board–vessel is about to proceed to sea'. For those female sailors, disguised as men, preparing to embark, this must have been a formidable moment, heralding their new life at sea.

Part One

Fantasy Figureheads
(Spirit of the Ship)

Women have traditionally appeared on ships and boats as the vessel figurehead, almost every prow having a carved figure looking down at the waves. Beautiful ornately carved sirens, brightly painted, and often gilded in real gold, became increasingly fashionable as a decorative feature on merchant ships during the eighteenth and nineteenth centuries. Life size idealised representations of handsome, buxom, strong women would elegantly drape the bow of a ship—importantly the outer side of the ship—bolted to the prow. The origin of ship figureheads goes back thousands of years. Sometimes an eye would be painted onto the bow of a ship by ancient civilisations. It is believed that figurehead tradition evolved from images of eyes aiding ship navigation during bad weather. Increasingly female figureheads were bare breasted metaphors depicting the mother image protecting and steering a ship through torrid seas. Sometimes representations of royal queens could be added to the bow in honour of an alleged strong, loyal woman supporting her seafarers. On smaller vessels carved depictions of wives or daughters were built into the boats' hardware to bring good luck to the roaming sailor. The objectification of women in the nautical sphere

The figurehead of *Cutty Sark* depicting the witch Nannie from Robert Burns's Tam O'Shanter. In the poem Nannie chases Tam, grabbing his horse's tail which comes off in her hand. Burns refers to Nannie's clothing as cutty-sark, which is an 18th-century Scottish term for a short chemise or underskirt.

was ritualised in the superstitious world of the male mariner. Allegories of topless women as figureheads were famously symbolic on pirate ships during the earlier sixteenth and seventeenth centuries. The establishment of a fashionable ship's figurehead, as a decorative accessory, was to become commonplace during the nineteenth century on many vessels.

Women are also traditionally assigned the role of ship's sponsor through the ritual of launching a ship; an important rite of passage for the ship-builders, and for the crew a blessing. The blessing of a ship with wine is thought to be a remnant of the Christian ritual of baptism. The matriarchal blessing of a ship, and importantly of all who sail in her, might represent a land based woman possessing a maternal and protective role over her sons. Indeed ships are still traditionally referred to as 'her' or 'she'.[5]

Figureheads went out of fashion with the rise of the military sailing ship. Changes in the construction, mainly with new preferred ram bows, meant that there was now no obvious place to mount a figurehead on battleships. Smaller vessels still carried scaled down versions of previous figureheads on their bows up till about World War I.[6]

Seadog Women
(Cross-dressing Women Sailors)

It sounds romantic: young women, girls, who ran away to sea in search of a life of adventure. It is easy to believe they just wanted to travel the world by living the life of a sailor. Another perspective might be that perhaps they were gender curious and wanted to explore the world of men at close quarters, and in some cases this was undoubtedly true. However, for the vast majority of women seafarers who were discovered, the truth appears to be a tale of fleeing an unhappy and desperate childhood, and only in a few cases are the women recorded in this work considered to be genuinely acting out transgenderism. A more mythical rationale to account for a woman taking such a drastic leap in her life was that she was even, in extreme cases, stalking a lost lover in her grief. Maritime folk lore, mainly in sea shanties, includes such examples of dispossessed females, which would have been passed on as oral history from man to man. The newspapers of the nineteenth century proliferated in the romanticised narrative of seafaring women dressed as men and such stories are explored in Part Two.

5   The National Maritime Museum suggests that the tradition relates to the idea of goddesses, other deities or members of a ship owner's family playing a protective role in looking after a ship and crew.
6   www.http://en.wikipedia.org/wiki/Figurehead

In large merchant ports such as Bristol hundreds of merchant ships sailing the world would have been moored up, quay side, offering a ready-made home from home. "The greatest, the richest, and the best port of trade in Great Britain, London only excepted"[7] At certain times of the year, the seaman would have seen as many as a thousand or more vessels, "their masts as thick as they can stand by one another."[8] At merchant ports ships would be sailing in and out continually when the tides allowed. But in naval ports, such as Portsmouth, the fleet would be away for long periods of time. When the fleet returned there would have been a carnival atmosphere as thousands of sailors disembarked. To many a young woman the thought of sailing the high seas must have been tempting–if only she could get away with it.

The men were now free—some hundreds of them at liberty to roam where they pleased—their pockets loaded with several years' pay, and the streets of Portsmouth were speedily filled with riot, intoxication, and disgusting revelry–fiddles playing, men and women dancing, from morning until night, and from night until morning; the whole street from Point to Sally Port in a state of uproar, and such disgraceful scenes hourly taking place, more than enough to shock the eyes of the uninitiated.[9]

Although life at sea was acutely physical, challenging and dangerous, a nautical existence did have benefits for our prospective seadog women.[10] A ship or boat provided shelter, a home of sorts; sailors would have their food rations guaranteed along with the all-important grog rations.[11] They had companionship, and were paid a reasonable wage at the end of the voyage. Before the twentieth century privateers and buccaneers received the spoils of their raids, sharing the booty among the crew and ship owners, in some

---

7   Alexander Pope in William Hunt. *Bristol.* London. 1895. pp. 175-176. Cited in Rediker M. *Between the Devil and the Deep Blue Sea. Merchant Seamen, Pirates and the Anglo-American Maritime World, 1700-1750.* Cambridge University Press. 1989. p.42.
8   Ibid.
9   A Blue Jacket, *Saucy Jack and the Indiaman.* Vol 1 London, 1840. 166. Cited in Beaven B. 'The resilience of sailortown culture in English naval ports, c.1820-1900'. *Urban History,* 43:1. 2016. p.79.
10   Seadog, slang for a sailor.
11   Grog, a drink traditionally made of rum mixed with water.

cases equally.[12] British naval crew also received a type of prize money from captured and salvaged enemy ships well into the twentieth century.[13]

Much of the time at sea would be spent doing ordinary ship's chores comprising of cleaning, continual repairs, recreation, sleeping, fishing, cooking and eating, with additional duties for those men serving on navy vessels. Remarkably William McDonald of Dundee was discovered in 1814 after sailing for five years in the merchant navy on the *David and Jean*. After falling overboard William was undressed to be put to bed to aid her recovery and hence her sex was discovered. Captain Lyle reported the women sailor in a letter to the ship owners.[14]

The reports of women who ran away to sea were commonly over-romanticised by newspaper stories at the time, with headings such as 'A Sea Romance, Girl ships as a Sailor' often connecting the woman–the heroine–as in flight for her man. However, what was forgotten is the fact that living the life of a sailor would enable a woman to have financial independence, and even led on to seafaring careers in some cases for the minority–so long as they remained undiscovered. Furthermore, and surprisingly, women serving in the navy in the disguise of men even petitioned after discovery for the right to receive a pension to which long serving and injured seamen were entitled. Much to the credit of the naval powers at the time is the fact that a few women did win their case for a service pension.

It is impossible to determine just how many women sailors disguised as men there have been across the centuries. It is plausible that only a small proportion of the women were ever found out, and we only know about those

12   A privateer ship would engage in warfare under a commission of war issued by the state and would not launch attacks on their own nation's vessels, or upon their own nation. Known as a letter of marque (the contract), the crew could attack and take a foreign ship as a prize. The captured ship would be sold off and the proceeds divided between the privateer sponsors, ship owners, officers and the crew. As a consequent, all merchant ships were armed, meaning the sailors were trained in sea warfare with merchant ships at times of war heavily subsidising the navies. Privateers were often no more than pirates and would take advantage of wars between nations. A 'letter of marque' was often issued hastily at times of war and privateers engaged in actions beyond the law of the issuing country. At the end of the nineteenth century the practice of issuing letters of marque fell out of favour because of the turmoil the practice caused by encouraging piracy. A privateer sailor acted independently, being only paid from the sharing out of the proceeds obtained from a captured enemy ship. This is an early example of privatisation by the state of the state-owned navy. Sir Francis Drake was a famous English privateer born in Plymouth in 1540. He combined commerce, warfare, slave trading and piracy with national defence, earning the royal coffers immense wealth and leading to Queen Elizabeth I promoting him to Vice Admiral.

13   This tradition was briefly carried on by the newly formed British Royal Air Force with the early pilots being granted the rights to occasional prize money.

14   *Caledonian Mercury*. 5 Feb. 1814.

who had biographies written about them, or appeared in newspaper reports. The true figure was probably a lot higher than recorded because an unknown number of cross-dressing women sailors were able to successfully carry out their plans, especially those women who took only one voyage to migrate and then deserted ship. By only committing to one sailing a woman was far less likely to be discovered. Sailors would carry forward stories they had heard about women in verse. There are examples of women sailors to be found in folk songs and sea shanties, which tell us their names and divulge why they came to run away to sea. The songs are highly romanticised, being based on an oral history circulated from sailor to sailor, and always from the male perspective—the woman as a victim, usually seeking out her lost lover.

Women sailors might also have been victims of cruel punishments meted out by officers. An example of a woman being flogged on board a naval ship can be found in the extraordinary life of Hannah Snell (1723-1792). After a brief unhappy marriage Hannah had a child after her husband, James Summes, deserted her. But her little girl, named Susannah, died aged only two. Following this tragedy she moved to Portsmouth in 1747, and disguised herself as a man, calling herself Bob Corigan, in an attempt to pursue her husband who was known to be in the army. Apparently Snell deserted the army following a brutal flogging of 500 lashes and joined the marines, serving on the *Swallow*, sailing to Lisbon, Mauritius and India. She was shot in the groin and legs 11 times during the battle of Devicottail in June 1749, but managed to avoid detection by asking a local woman to remove the bullet instead of the ship's surgeon. After serving for over five years she learned that her first husband had been killed so she left the navy on 2 June 1750, after disclosing her true sex to her shipmates. Snell then petitioned the Duke of Cumberland, the head of the army, for her pension, which was begrudgingly granted in November 1750, and increased in 1785, which was very unusual. After retiring, Hannah married again and kept a pub in Southwark, London for a short time. She married three times in total, having two sons, and died on 8 February 1792 in Bethlem Lunatic Hospital, probably due to syphilis. Her biography *The Female Soldier* was first published in 1750.[15] Incidentally, another example of a woman sailor being ordered to be flogged was Charles Waddall, a naval seaman who was found to be a woman when she was stripped for a flogging in 1781.

15   *Hannah Snell*. http://en.m.wikipedia.org/Hannah_Snell

HANNAH SNELL,
the Female Soldier,
Who went by the Name of James Gray.

Ingenious Schemes to Look like a Man.

How could a female get away with cross-dressing and hiding her sex when surrounded by men, and in such close quarters below deck? There are records of male sailors going to tailors and having fancy jackets run up, adorned with lace and gold buttons. It was not until the late nineteenth century that naval seamen were issued with formal uniforms, as a symbol of nationality. Sailors would purchase their own often elaborate and refined clothing that would be worn for the duration of a voyage. This was one way in which sailors would spend their pay that they received on return to port. In Plymouth it was noted that sailors, using their pay-off, created an informal uniform using 'the finest broadcloths'[16] of scarlet velvet with lace trimmings and perforated guineas sewn on as buttons, with white trousers trimmed with a gold fringe.[17] Sailors might even treat themselves to a powdered wig when they were fashionable, and live the life of an urban gentleman during shore-leave if they received generous prize money. Shore-leave offered a means of escapism to enjoy briefly the offerings of sailortown in style and merriment, having once again escaped from long confinement on board ship. However, for most sailors their everyday 'uniform' was a practical affair made up of loose fitting canvas trousers, a tight blue jacket, and a hat of some kind, worn throughout a voyage and then re-purchased on return to a port. Facial hair would have been visible as men would normally only shave twice a week while at sea, unless beards were in fashion, so for our sailor women a lack of facial hair must have been potentially problematic.

Before the 1920s male and female clothing was strictly demarcated to distinguish and separate the sexes. For women the bosom was pushed up and corsets were worn, thereby accentuating her gender specific characteristics. So that at the slightest of glances, perhaps on an unlit street, or in the darkness of below decks, it was almost impossible not to be able to identify a female on sight. Take away the clearly defined two-gender dress code, and it would have been very difficult to differentiate between male and female, and not immediately obvious that a person was cross-dressing. After all, in the everyday, society did not expect a person to cross-dress, or even suspect that it happened, unless they were attending the music hall or a theatre house where women entertainers frequently dressed up as men.

16 Broadcloth is a dense, plain woven fabric, usually made of wool. Yarns were shrunk to make the dense weave closer thereby making the cloth highly weather-resistant and hard wearing, perfect for working on deck in all weathers.
17 Beaven B. 'The resilience of sailortown culture in English naval ports, c.1820-1900'. *Urban History*, 43:1. 2016. p.79.

Hair styling for male sailors was often one of longish hair, plaited at the back, perhaps tied with a plain ribbon, or cut short, depending on the era. Women on the other hand had very elaborate hair styles. Hair was always kept long and usually worn up in great piles on top of the head. Brightly coloured ribbons and combs were employed to hold the hair in place. Another fashion accessory to separate women from men was the wearing of hats. Although men wore hats they would be made of a plain material of a practical nature and designed to either designate their class in society or professional rank, or simply to keep them warm and dry. By contrast female hats were worn as a statement of added attractiveness; being highly decorated for those that could afford it and usually completely impractical!

Many boys were on board ships working as cabin boys, learning the sailors' trade; it was common for their careers to commence at the age of eleven. Obviously the boys would not have had facial or body hair, so for a young woman it could actually be relatively easy to pass as a boyish man. Being of slighter build a younger woman would have had this in her favour, not forgetting that the average man before the modern era was significantly shorter in stature than men today. Roderick Floud et al. analysed the changes in heights of poor boys recruited by the Marine Society of London between 1770 and 1870 and those recruited by the Royal Marines and the British Army between 1740 and 1914. The study showed a gradual increase in height, with the exception of height falling temporarily during 1840 and 1850.[18] The data suggested that although height fluctuated during the century, from the 1840s onwards there was an upward trend on average. However, during the same period fourteen year old boys from wealthier families attending the Royal Military Academy at Sandhurst were nearly six inches taller than their counterparts attending the Marine Society. Boys from rural areas were slightly taller than those from urban backgrounds, suggesting that environmental factors such as disease, overcrowding, poor nutrition and pollution were influencing growth rates. Floud concluded that the discrepancy in male heights was due directly to 'significant differences in the heights of men and boys from different socioeconomic backgrounds'.[19] Although there is considerably less data on the stature of girls, Floud assumes from data collected on school children in the early twentieth century, that in past generations girls may have been slightly taller than boys.[20] Considering that most ordinary sailors were

18   1840-1850 was the decade known as the Hungry Forties across Europe, due mainly to Potato Blight disease. The consequence was a mass failure of the crop. In England, although less affected, many thousands of working class people starved to death.
19   Floud R. et al. *Height, health and history: Nutritional status in the United Kingdom 1750-1980*. Cambridge University Press. 1990.
20   Ibid. p.17.

from working class backgrounds, and therefore shorter than the average, and that females were on average slightly taller than males, height may not have differed much between them. This factor, along with cross-dressing, would have contributed to women sailors accomplishing a near perfect disguise, and therefore making them far less likely to be suspected.

As mentioned previously, a woman's hair could be cut off to make her appear male, and women disclosed on being found out that they had bound their breasts with a sheet of cloth as necessary. A quilted or padded jacket, as sourced by one woman sailor to hide her female form, would be worn in some cases over bound breasts. Sailors wore loose fitting trousers, often made of canvas, so this would be an advantage to easily hide female broader hips and lack of body hair.

Other practicalities of everyday life for women such as the monthly cycle, and going to the toilet, might have been an issue within the context of our modern day familiarity of female biology. It is probable that on the whole men (and in particular sailors who spent little time with women), would have been ignorant of a woman's monthly menstruation. We must remember that this was a taboo subject until very recently; women would even hide evidence of their monthly cycle from their husbands. Another factor to take into consideration is that with a lack of contraception women were more frequently pregnant than today, therefore menstruation, absent while pregnant and often naturally absent when breast-feeding, would have been a far less frequent event for many women. Therefore, one can only surmise that if a woman sailor in male disguise was discovered throwing a blooded rag over board this could simply be explained away by an illness or injury to the nether regions as may have been suffered by male sailors. Toilet facilities would have been more difficult as sailors urinated over the side of a ship. We can only assume that women sailors would, with difficultly, find privacy to use the head (a primitive toileting hole over the bow of a ship which emptied straight into the water), or a chamber pot or similar, and might even pretend to urinate directly into the sea. We simply do not know, as there appears to be nothing written about this characteristic of their intimate lives recorded in the biographies of women sailors; this aspect of their life is no more than speculation on the part of historians.

Another difficultly for the women is that sailors lived at very close quarters to each other below deck, with often only 18 inches of designated space to sling their hammocks on crowded warships. Sailors would sleep in their clothing, rarely if ever washing these items or, needless to say, their bodies. There must have been an attitude of live and let live between the crew regarding physical body issues, each to their own, minding their own business; no looking, no touching, would have been the only way to tolerate the cramped and smelly living conditions when it came to intimate space.

For how long the women could get away with cross-dressing to work as a man is quite another matter, as history only discloses to us those women that were discovered. It is a fact that many women successfully managed to emigrate disguised as male sailors, earning and saving enough money to start a new life.

Sailortown Women
(Economic Survival on the Shoreline)

We'll spend our money merrily,
When we come home from sea;
With every man, a glass in his hand
And a pretty girl on his knee.

Some women have always enjoyed travel. However, in the past it was only very rarely that perhaps a well-to-do spinster of independent means would have had the opportunity to travel and experience sailing the seas, usually as a first class passenger. An interest in botany or in the arts would give the 'lady' an air of bourgeois respectability. For example, at the age of 50, following the death of her parents, Adela Breton, a 'gentlewoman', left her comfortable life in Bath during 1899 to sail to Mexico. She became a respected explorer and artist. Breton bequeathed more than 1,500 of her artworks to the Bristol Museum and Art Gallery, where they are still archived.[21] Women from the middling classes (the middle classes) would also sail as missionaries to the colonies, again with an air of entitlement. Sometimes officers would allow their wives to accompany them, even on man-of-war ships in battle. For industrial ships such as whalers it was actually traditional for captains' wives to live with their husbands on board. They would work on board the whaler, cooking and nursing. But for some women of free spirit with little or no money, education or prospects, their only chance to break free was to disguise themselves as men-boys in order to take up traditional male occupations. They would have witnessed sailors arriving back from what were often very long voyages with fists full of money and exotic tales from afar. Women and children who lived on or near to large docks or small fishing ports would have had a practical knowledge of the sea and its dangers with continual tales of life at sea being recounted at home by the fireside. Sadly, for many families sailors would never return home.

21   Duffus J. *Women Who Built Bristol 1184-2018.* Tangent Books. 2018. p. 395. Ibid. p.59.

Men who worked locally on the water, such as bargemen and pilots, were also supported by women; a tightly bonded community, with both men and women heavily reliant on the other to protect their way of life. For example, the women of Pill on the River Avon near Bristol thought nothing of using violence during labour disputes to defend the men who worked as pilots. Detailed by Mike Richardson in *Pirates to Proletarians*[22], the following account of a violent assault conducted by the resilient women of Pill upon turncoat pilot Richard Case, resulting in the unfortunate Case being tarred and 'floured', appeared in the *Bristol Mercury and Daily Post*, on the 10th March 1881:

Richard Arthur Case, son of Richard Case, pilot, said he worked for his father. The previous Thursday witness assisted his father in taking the steamer *Gloucester* from Avonmouth to Bristol. They returned to Pill in a boat, which contained witness, his father, John Case, Henry Case, James Ellis, and William Hook. Having landed witness's father at Shirehampton, they rowed across the river to the slip at Pill. On reaching this a crowd of boys and girls ran down the slip, headed by a man named Percival, and tried to haul the boat up. The three male defendants jumped into the boat and challenged witness to fight, but he declined to do so. Frank and Sidney Smith then thrust their fists into his face, and Williams struck him twice on the head. They then tried to throw him overboard, and some one from the shore called out for them to pitch him into the river. At the time the tide was running down strong. Sidney and Frank Smith seized hold of him, and said they would throw him over. He was forced down in the struggle so much that a coat he had on his arm went into the water. Witness succeeded in getting on the shore, and William Smith seized him by the collar when about three-parts of the way up the ship. Mrs. Summers then came up and threw a quantity of flour over him, and shortly after Sidney Smith struck him. (Witness here produced the clothes which he was wearing at the time, and said the marks on them were occasioned by the tar and flour thrown over him.) Stones and mud were then thrown by the crowd, and witness received a wound at the back of his head, and when he came to apply for the summons he had a piece of skin knocked off his face. A swelling also came up in his back, which

---

22   For the full story of the boat pilots of Pill attacking merchant captains, with the support of the women, see Mike Richardson *Pirates to Proletarian. The Experience of the Pilots and Waterman of Crockerne Pill in the Nineteenth Century*. Bristol Radical Pamphleteer. Pamphlet #23. 2012.

he attributed to being forced across the gunwale of the boat by the male defendants shelter in the Red Lion-court, and Sidney Smith followed him in and again assaulted him. A pilot named Batlay brought the *Gloucester* from Lundy to Avonmouth.

Jane Summers and Emma Dickins were charged with assault and each given fines of forty shillings, costs and fourteen days imprisonment with hard labour. Richard Case was reviled by the Pill pilot families because he represented the 'capitalization' of the docks.[23] The Great Western Steamship Company decided to employ pilots directly for their larger ships. Before this time the pilots of the Severn Estuary, the gateway to the port of Bristol, had worked for centuries as independent operators and would race to greet and guide ships along the treacherous mud flats and tides of the Severn. The Pill pilots were on strike because new working practices were threatening their livelihoods and hence the wider community of Pill. Local people protested along the Pill shoreline during the dispute, heckling Great Western ships and their crews. Women and children carried effigies of the complicit Western pilots around the village of Pill and torched them overlooking the river so they would be visible to other sailors passing by.[24]

Sailortown was, and is, a constructed space of social and material consumerism with institutional and economic forces forging lives and spatial interdependencies upon the people who lived in these towns. Nautical trade was paramount to the survival of the women and their families who occupied these coastal districts. These were places containing unique communities of distinct cultures that were different from land-locked populations. The people of sailortowns engaged with a maritime economy where the pace of work was significantly altered compared to land based commerce. Individual ships could arrive suddenly or en masse as naval fleets arrived or departed; merchant ports operated at a more even pace dependent on the timings of the twice daily tides which usually controlled sailing schedules.

Although a busy, noisy and colourful space, life was often one of hardship and drudgery for many working class girls and women. They had little or no choices in how they were to live their lives, with confinement to the domestic sphere usually their only option. Romantic literature satisfied the fantasies of the middling classes of young women, those of marrying a prince or at least a handsome, well-thought-of young man to take them away from a life of servitude. The few options available for unmarried working class females, who

---

23   Poole S. ed. *A City Built Upon the Water. Maritime Bristol 1750-1900.* Redcliffe Press. 2013. p.74
24   *Bristol Mercury.* 9 Dec. 1890.

were frequently illiterate[25], included domestic service, agricultural labouring, weaving, preserving and selling fish, seamstress, laundress, coal hurrier[26], or within the new industrialised world working in a cotton mill or with other mechanised processes. Work in factories was very demanding and owners expected long hours of the women employees at up to fourteen hours a day. Pay was low and they endured terrible working conditions with absolutely no workers' rights. Before the Mines and Collieries Act of 1842 women and children were allowed to work below ground in mines. The Act banned all women, girls and boys less than ten years of age from working underground.[27] Although the Act was certainly needed, the unintended consequence for many women and children was to leave them without any alternative work and therefore destitute.

Vagrancy had become very prevalent across Britain during the mid-eighteenth century due to economic slump and traditional farm labourers migrating into the cities seeking work and charity. Bristol was no exception. Vagrants in Bristol were sent to the workhouse, whipped and put to hard labour. A vagrant was considered a woman, man or child, who was begging, singing songs or playing music in the streets, sleeping outdoors, or engaging in prostitution, to give a few examples. Between 1786 and 1787, in Bristol alone, at least eighty-one vagrants were named, examined, whipped and taken to the workhouse. Of these persons twenty four were from Bristol parishes, many of them being women, some as young at twelve years of age, who each received twelve lashes for being 'on the town'.[28]

Riot and Rebellion in Sailortowns

Sailortown women were up in arms during 1771 when the 'chip-women' of Portsmouth were not allowed access to the ship yard, resulting in them rioting in protest.[29] What were chips? And, more importantly why were they so valuable and perceived as a 'right' to the women?

25   Illiteracy rates were at approximately 50% at this time and higher among females.
26   A woman, or worse still a child, was tied with a harness like strap to a cart in order to haul the mined coal along narrow railway tracks to the mine surface, in dark underground corridors and often in tiny low spaces.
27   In 1841 an estimated 216,000 people were employed in the mines. Women and children worked underground for 12 hours a day for lower wages than men. As there was no compensation for those who lost their jobs, and only one inspector for the whole of Britain, it is suspected that some women and children continued to work illegally in the mines after the passing of the 1842 Act.
28   Poole. S. & Rogers. N. *Bristol from Below. Law, Authority and Protest in a Georgian City.* The Boydell Press. 2017. p.66.
29   Linebaugh. op. cit. p.378

Chips, or chippings, did not merely mean small wood-chips as the connotation is today, but for shipyard workers, and those who lived close to the dockyards, they represented the long held customary right to collect a certain amount of timber and other items surplus to requirements such as nails and rope. In fact chips were any items that were used in the construction of wooden ships, with the right being enshrined by law since 1634 for workers and locals to take them home. Chips mainly consisted of small wood off-cuts no longer than three feet in length, although other scraps or various metals might also be concealed within the bundles of wood and carried out of the ship yard. The amount of chips that could be harvested was generally fixed as any tied up bundle that could be carried under one arm, or sometimes the amount that could be carried over one shoulder, depending on the ship yard and era. Over the years many attempts were made by the navy to reduce the amount of timber wastage lost to employees. Draconian measures were introduced, such as attempting to reduce the amount of chips that could physically be carried out of the yards by changing the rules to reduce the size of the bundles.

During 1739 Deptford naval dockyard workers went out on strike because the navy attempted to reduce night and tide work, but equally as important was an attempt to reduce the number of chips the men and women could take out of the yard. It was proposed that chips should be unbundled and only carried under the arm, instead of being tied up and carried over the shoulder, thus reducing the amount that could be taken out from the shipyard. In April 1768 shipwrights at Chatham naval dockyard fought the marines over 'a Bundle of Chips' as was their 'custom' to leave the yard with each day. Magistrates were summoned to read the Riot Act to the men, and, on hearing this, strikers declared, 'we will not tamely suffer ourselves to be made slaves to any particular man's whim, *for we are free-born subjects*'.[30] The true value and freedom to gather chips had become symbolic of a new found and non-traditional link with working class ideals; epitomising the concepts of freedom, the rights of man, equality, and the wrongs of slavery.

The right to take chippings out of the yard was a continual cause of disagreement on the part of the Admiralty, who believed the right was being taken advantage of by the workers and local women. The Admiralty did adhere to a call for an increase in labour wages while at the same time attempting to stop the practice of chipping, but the labourers just took the increase in wages and continued to remove chips. What is more, chips were a legal part of dockyard workers' pay, and although cash pay rates remained

---

30   Ranft. B.M. 'Labour Relations in the Royal Dockyards in 1739', *The Mariner's Mirror*, Vol. xxxiii, No.4. Jan. 1926. Cited in Linebaugh. op. cit.

low and non-negotiable, chips were used as a bargaining tool by both sides. The question arises as to what exactly was the navy going to do with these small off-cuts that were surplus to requirements? It is dubious to believe that it had any practical use for them. Chips were fundamental to the survival of the local economy in naval sailortowns where ships were being built and repaired. Deptford workers and women said that they could not live without the right to chips, as their wages were so low. It is no coincidence that local housing had staircase steps constructed at precisely three feet wide and that doors, cupboards and other features in local housing were all made up of pieces of timber three feet long or under. This peculiarity was observed by Sir Samuel Bentham in 1795, who was living next to the Portsmouth yard gatehouse.[31] Chips were also an essential free source of fuel for fires, enabling bathing and cooking for example, and therefore contributing to the health and welfare of the local people to compensate for low wages. Women's work at home would have relied on the procurement of chips so they could earn money by taking in laundry and cooking foodstuffs for sale on the streets, in fact any cottage industry that required fuel.

By 1767 pamphlets were being distributed claiming the 'many evils' arising from 'upwards of two thousand, mostly Women' who entered the dockyards on Wednesdays and Saturdays (as was their right), 'to take from thence the small Chips and Gleanings of the Yard'. Twice a week small chips and sweepings were dumped at the yard gates so that women could gather the off-cuts but they were not able to enter the yard itself.[32] The Admiralty had initiated yet another campaign—this time aimed specifically at the women. The rights to chips were once again being used as a bargaining tool over wage disputes during a time of inflation.

At Plymouth dockyards, as elsewhere, the men were fed by their womenfolk, who would bring food into the yard twice a day. However, the women were observed to be bringing out chips, along with off-cuts of pieces of iron and nails, in the baskets they had delivered the food in. Although the gate porter was instructed to stop the women carrying baskets into the yard, he confessed that, "I don't know how to get at a mode of affecting it".[33] A warden in an attempt to prevent three women coming into the yard reported to the Navy Board during a crackdown on chipping in 1783 that "[The women] behaved so outrageously that he was obliged to give one of them a

31   Bentham M.S. *The Life of Brigadier-General Sir Samuel Bentham*. Cited in Linebaugh. op. cit.
32   Linebaugh. op. cit. p.379. 1862.
33   Wright R.J.B. '*The Royal Dockyards in England at the time of the American War of Independence*'. PhD dissertation. London University. 1972. p.184

shove with a broom by which she fell down". The women's determination to enter the dockyards indicates that their right to chippings was a fundamental and deep-seated belief in their entitlement to off-cuts, and was a legitimate source of income to be defended.[34]

Employment Opportunities for Sailortown Women

With few employment options for single women, and many women being poverty-stricken through no fault of their own, their options were limited. The poor relief system was not usually available for women without children unless they were incapacitated in some way. Impoverished single men, on the other hand, could easily become sailors if they were healthy, giving them a home on board a ship and food rations. But for women this was not an option, leaving them with very limited opportunities for work in times of economic depression and high unemployment.

Prostitution was one source of employment, particularly for those women who during times of famine had left behind the protection of a familiar rural community to move to the towns in search of work during the Industrial Revolution. The profession did give the luckier ones an independence of sorts for women requiring money quickly, as sailortowns guaranteed a high turnover of clients.[35] One benefit would have been shorter working hours than in the factories, with higher pay and a social life. Contrary to common belief, women were allowed to stay on board when sailing around British ports so for some prostitutes in sailortowns the profession might have also given them the possibility to sail on a ship and relocate at another port. According to historian and writer Susanne Stark, sailors would often quickly marry a prostitute while on shore leave in 'quick–marriage' chapels located in sailortowns because their shore leave was brief and the men wanted to have a home while in port and on future occasions.[36]

The census of 1821 reveals that 4,798 more females than males were living in the combined ports of Portsmouth and Portsea, of which many

34   Ibid. p.199

35   It is impossible to estimate the numbers of women (and men) working as prostitutes because women who lived unmarried with a man, or single mothers living alone, for example, would sometimes be branded as a prostitute. However, in London in 1790 it was estimated that 50,000 prostitutes were working in the dock parishes and Covent Garden district. This figure cannot be substantiated but is an estimate taken from various diaries and newspaper letters to editors during the era. Needless to say the figure would be high.

36   Unpublished journal, 'Samuel Stokes, 1806-1807 and 1809-1815: His Life in the Merchant and Royal Navies.' Cited in Stark S.J. *Female Tars. Women aboard ship in the age of sail*. Pimlico, London. 1998. p.32.

were sailors' wives. However, Stark points out that the wives of seamen waiting transportation to their home parishes were not counted on the census. Seaman Samuel Stokes wrote that on pay day in 1809 on the 98-gun *Dreadnought* with 800 men on board, the ship was visited in port by nearly 1,000 women, with only 50 of them being wives.[37] We can conclude that there was no shortage of women plying their wares at the ports when the fleet came home. The work would not always lead to a physical sexual encounter as there would also be a hostess only role. But why would women choose to be prostitutes, in an age when they risked catching incurable diseases, unwanted pregnancies, robbery, rape and cruel treatment by some members of crew? Pay rates were very low for women who worked in small industries on piecework[38], making it very difficult for them to live off their earnings if living alone, or single with children. For some women with children it was an unambiguous choice of prostitution or the workhouse. Begging was another option but was illegal under the Vagrancy Laws whereas prostitution was semi-legal.

Ann Smith of Bristol was unlucky in marriage, and due to an absent sailor husband and lack of employment opportunities she fell on hard times. Ann was suspected of vagrancy when walking the streets of St Nicholas in Bristol during January 1773. Although she had settlement rights by marriage in the then village of Brislington (now a suburb of Bristol) her husband 'went to sea, since which she has never seen him or heard from him, nor does she know whether he is living or dead'. Ann had been abandoned by her husband perhaps through illness and being off loaded at another port, or through his desertion. She was left alone with her two illegitimate children conceived before she married and another child of a year old from her marriage.[39] Her only limited employment was occasional domestic service and agricultural labouring in Brislington, which would have been very limited with three young children to care for.

Another story, detailed below, was recounted by a woman from the dock region of the East End of London, and clearly demonstrates the consequences of finding herself entrapped into poverty. The narrative is just one selected from thousands of similar accounts from women with similar experiences, documented by social reformers in order to record the effects of poverty on the lives of the working classes.

---

37   Ibid.
38   Workers are paid for a 'piece' of completed work regardless of the time required to produce an item.
39   BA, P.St LB/OP/13 (*St Lukes, Brislington, vagrancy examinations*), *Examination of Ann Smith, 22 Jan. 1773*. Cited in Poole. S. & Rogers N. op. cit. p.67.

On December 1, 1839 the *Western Times; Exeter* ran an article entitled "Labour and the Poor".[40]

Magdalen…was a tall, fine grown girl, with remarkably regular features. She told her tale, with her face hidden in her hands, and sobbing…"I used to work at slop-work[41]—at the shirt work—the fine full-fronted white shirts: I got 2 1/4d [old pennies] each for 'em. There were six button-holes, four rows of stitching in the front, and the collars and wristbands stitched as well. By working from five o-clock in the morning till midnight each night, I might be able to do seven in the week. These would bring me in 17 1/2d for my whole weeks labour. Out of this the cotton must be taken and that came to 2d every week…[the rest] to pay rent and living and buy candles with…It was impossible for me to live. I was forced to go out of a night to make out me living. I had a child, and it used to cry for food…I left my child at home wrapped in a bit of old blanket, while I went out…I went on to the streets solely to get a living for myself and child…I am the daughter of a minister of the gospel…He died when I was eight…It was the low price for my labour that drove me to prostitution…we used to sit in a shed, for I was too fatigued with my baby to stand…One night, in the depth of winter, his legs froze to my side. I was trying to make my way to the workhouse, but was so weak I couldn't get on any farther. [I tried begging]. The snow was over my shoes…We hadn't tasted any food since the morning before…A lady saw me sitting on the door-step, and took me into her house, and rubbed my child's legs with brandy. She gave us some food…but I was too far gone to eat. I got to the workhouse that night. I told them we were starving, but they refused to admit us without an order; so I went back to prostitution for another month. [Eventually] I got an order for the workhouse, and went in there for two years. The very minute we got inside the gate they took my child away from me, and allowed me to see it only once a month…I and another left "the house" to work at umbrella covering, so that we might have our children with us…the work wasn't to [sic] bad. I then made from 3s to 4s a-week, [note: 20 shillings to a British pound] and from that I gave up prostitution.

40 *Western Daily Times.* 1 Dec. 1849. 'A Thrilling Narrative' (From the Reports of "Labour and the Poor", in *The Morning Chronicle).* p.5
41 Cheap ready-made clothing.

This was the harsh reality of the stark choices that some women had to make in life to survive in eighteenth and nineteenth century England. Magdalen clearly was a skilled seamstress, who was willing to work hard, but her sewing simply did not pay enough for her and her child to live independently and keep them out of the workhouse. In the early 1840s the working classes, lower middle class and 'distressed gentlewomen' were increasingly being put in a position of having to support themselves and their families due to high male unemployment. Also, sailors would be away from home for many months, often several years, and were only paid on their return, causing financial hardship for their families, leaving the women to take in work at home.

Millinery and dressmaking were considered respectable occupations and suitably feminine. It was one of the few occupations that offered a skill accredited to women, a sense of belonging to a trade, and furthermore apprenticeships were being undertaken by girls and young women even at this time. The growing middle classes had caused a demand for ready-made men's clothing, which was cheaper to buy than using traditional tailors. This meant that working class women could work from the home, so that they could watch over their children and still manage necessary domestic chores. But this convenience also meant they were exploited by only receiving very low piece work rates. Sewing men's shirts, even for starvation wages, was often preferable as it allowed women to remain independent when their men were at sea while still ensuring the stereotypical roles of wives and mothers were observed.[42] The women were also still reliant on earnings from sailor's wages, money that they might have to wait years for, and in the meantime earning 'pin money',[43] working from the home or worse. For

42   The low paid labouring seamstress is an occupation that epitomises sweatshop labour throughout the world then and still, sadly, today. In England, the famous Dagenham Women's Strike was brought about by a sisterhood of collective women who were fed up with being paid far less than their male colleagues doing comparable work. In 1968, 850 women working as sewing machinists at the Ford Motor Company's plant in Dagenham, Essex twice went on strike over equal pay rights. The women were also on strike because the patriarchal unions at the time were not interested in representing them because they did not take the issue of women's right to equal pay seriously. At the time women who went out to work in factories were deemed to be working for 'pin money', in other words they were only working to be able to pay for life's small luxuries; the work place outside the home was still being perceived in the ownership of the male sphere. The continuing attitude towards women's work in that it should be hidden was as familiar to the Dagenham women as it would have been to Magdalen. After being on strike for six weeks a compromise was reached following government intervention. Two years later the Equal Pay Act 1970 came into law, considered a victory for working women.

43   The term 'pin money' originally was a small allowance given to women by their husbands to purchase items like clothing and basic essentials. Now the word is a derogatory term for women earning very low wages.

centuries women, including sailors' women, were hidden in the family unit and thus obscured from struggles for citizens' rights and workers' rights. Solidarity between women was an early feminist theme, often to be found in sailortowns.

During 1843 a report was published named the 'Second Report of the Children's Employment Commission'.[44] The public were shocked with horror stories of the cruel and heartless exploitation of needlewomen housed in the backrooms of London, leading to many letters being written to newspaper editors. The report revealed how some women, including sailors' wives, succumbed to the dangers of street prostitution to feed their children. The 'distressed seamstress' accounts would resurface at times of civil unrest, claiming that the breakdown of working class families was upon society because the pay for women was too low. The era of the 'hungry forties', as the 1840s became known, saw Britain facing a national crisis of civil unrest, and offered a perfect example of Benjamin Disraeli's later 'Two Nations', a massive division in wealth and power between rich and poor.[45] According to Peter Lindert, women's wages either stagnated or declined as a percentage of male wages between 1750 and 1820, and rose less rapidly than male wage rates between 1820 and 1950.[46] This was due partly to the demarcation and nature of female employment, and variants in occupational restrictions imposed upon women in the home during the nineteenth century in particular.

For many sailors a sort of bachelor life was the best compromise for the reality of being away at sea for months and often years at a time. They would set up home with single women who were sometimes prostitutes in their home port, or in other ports where they disembarked. The tradition was to pay the women in advance for months, (traditionally half their

44   Harris B. "Slaves of the Needle" The Seamstress in the 1840's. *The Victorian Web* www.victorianweb.org

45   Disraeli Benjamin. *Sybil, Or the Two Nations*. Oxford University Press 1998. p. 172. Originally published in 1845. 1. "Two nations, between whom there is no intercourse and no sympathy; who are as ignorant of each other's habits, thoughts, and feelings, as if they were dwellers in different zones, or inhabitants of different planets; who are formed by a different breeding, are fed by a different food, are ordered by different manners, and are not governed by the same laws—THE RICH AND THE POOR." p. 66. Also: 2. "There is more serfdom in England now than at any time since the Conquest, I speak of what passes under my daily eyes when I say, that those who labour can as little choose or change their masters now, as when they were born thralls. There are great bodies of the working classes of this country nearer the condition of brutes." Disraeli.

46   Lindert P. 1994.' Unequal living standards'. *The economic history of Britain since 1700*. Vol.1:357. p.86. Cambridge University Press.

THE LAST JIG or ADIEU TO OLD ENGLAND.

The Last Jig or Adieu to Old England by Thomas Rowlandson, 1818.

wages). In return women would keep a home with shore-life comforts ready for the sailor to enjoy when he came back to port. There would often be a practical agreement between the couple that while the man was away at sea the woman could and would entertain other men. These women often had children, either from a previous marriage or by their sailor partners. Victorian reformer and social researcher Henry Mayhew witnessed these arrangements in London's sailortowns. One prostitute told him that: "I know very many sailors—six, eight, then oh! More than that. They are my husbands. I am not married, of course not, but they do think me their wife whilst they are on shore." The woman added that she looked after their money as "It [is] very bad for [a] sailor to keep his money himself; he will fall into bad hands."[47]

Sailortowns had a higher rate of illegitimate children than inland towns. Estimates put the figure during the mid-nineteenth century at one in ten children being born outside of marriage within the parishes that ran along the shore lines of sea ports, including the Bristol Docks, although in reality the figure might have been higher than this. As referred to previously, prostitution was one option to which some women had to

47   Quoted in Burton V. 'The work and home life of seafarers, with special reference to the port of Southampton, 1870-1921'. *London School of Economics.* PhD theses. 1988. p.285

resort to survive. This may have resulted in higher numbers of illegitimate children in the parishes surrounding docklands and naval ports. But for others, an unquantifiable number, there was a different course of action to be taken for economic survival. These women chose instead to secretly, by way of a male disguise, switch gender roles and apply to join a ship. Although probably quite rare, nautical women certainly had an impact on those around them if they were discovered.

Women who wanted to achieve their life ambition but found themselves held back by cultural exclusion would occasionally resort to dressing as a man in other areas of employment too. For example, there were women who dressed as men to enter the male space of medical school. James Barry is one such example. He was said to be bad-tempered and a squeaky-voiced eccentric. He was frequently teased by his colleagues for his voice and challenged his tormentors to duels, shooting one man dead through the lung![48] Barry was born in Ireland, her true name being Margaret Ann Buckley. Her family were revolutionaries with Venezuelan connections, with her uncle, General Francisco De Miranda, becoming the leader of Venezuela. The plan was that Margaret would enter Edinburgh University, dressed as a man, to study medicine and then, following graduation, to practice medicine as a woman in Venezuela. Barry successfully studied medicine at the university from 1809 to 1812, and then went on to practice medicine across the world, often on board ships, becoming a distinguished army surgeon. Remarkably she ended her career as Inspector General of military hospitals. It was only when she died of dysentery in 1865 that her maid discovered her true sex as she was laying her out for her funeral. Barry's life undoubtedly demonstrates the lengths and ease with which women were able to successfully disguise their persona as men, something which Margaret Ann Buckley managed to achieve for all of her adult life.

An Entrepreneurial Spirit

Women as wives, daughters and extended family worked on the shoreline and in sailortowns, supporting their families while their men folk were at sea. On the sailors' return, the women saw to their injuries, sewed their clothes, cooked wholesome food and no doubt listened to their tales of great battles or the exotic countries they sailed to. The women mended fishing nets, made ropes for anchors and rigging, made and repaired sailor clothing, unloaded the catch or produce, harvested shellfish, acted

48   Barry J. *College of Medicine & Veterinary Medicine. The University of Edinburgh*. 2018. https://www.ed.ac.uk/medicine-vet-medicine/about/history/women/james-barry

as nurses, opened their houses as lodgings for shore leave sailors, and ran coffee houses, brothels and inns. Women also kept guard and fought off the notorious press gangs as a defensive collective, protecting local men from being impressed into the British navy.

Women would sell goods and provisions to sailors and visitors on the quay side. This must have been a very jolly time with dancing in the inns, sailors enjoying their freedom. In return sailors would entertain their sweethearts with exotic goods; valuables were carefully packaged away for the long voyage home as gifts, such as ornate glassware or china, fancy toys for their children, often crafted by the sailors on long voyages, or even captured wild animals such as parrots and monkeys, and even the odd tiger!

Mariner William Spavens writes in 1759 of how, when he was anchored at St John's, Antigua in the West Indies, local women would set up a market on board the ship to provide the men with much needed fresh food and other provisions. The men, many of whom were impressed, would not have been allowed to go ashore for fear by the officers that they might desert, so the enterprising women came to them. Spavens writes:

This harbour being free from sharks...the Negro women, having sugar, sugar-canes, fish, greens, yams, potatoes, oranges, plantains, bananas, pine-apples, cashue nuts, scalions, casava bread, prickly pears...to bring on board...they will...put their several commodities together, with what little apparel they wear, into a half tub; then launching it off the shore, they will swim after it, pushing it on before them till they come along side...receiving help from some of the crew, they get their goods on board; then dry and dress themselves, and stand their market till they have sold their articles. They then again undress, deposit their clothes in the tub, launch it overboard, jump after it, and return ashore.[49]

In the sailortowns of Britain some women would offer sexual services to visiting sailors on board ship while it was at anchor. Small craft, known as bumboats, transported wives, girlfriends and prostitutes alike to the waiting ships and the women could, and often did, stay on board for the duration of the ship being in port, for months in some cases! According to maritime historian David Cordingly, "women often owned the bumboats that were rowed out" to the eagerly waiting ships. The women would load

49   Spavens W., Rodger N.A.M ed. *Memoirs of a Seafaring Life. The Narrative of William Spavens. Pensioner on the Naval Chest at Chatham.* The Bath Press, Bath. For the members of The Folio Society MM 2000, pp.165-166. 1796.

SEA STORES.

Sea Stores by Thomas Rowlandson, 1812. The prostitute in the middle holds
out her hand for payment, while the sailor fumbles in his pocket for change.

them up like floating market stalls with all sorts of food produce, much needed tobacco and alcohol, as well as fancy goods to meet the needs of any women who were on board. The fare for being rowed out to the waiting ships was paid by the sailors, who were at liberty to choose which women were to come on board. The numbers on board a ship, in port, could amount to up to a thousand persons. Women would mainly stay below decks, finding a space in hammocks crammed in and between the ship's guns and crew chests, which must have been very uncomfortable and problematic; the noise and stench must have been appalling.[50] The old nautical saying 'show a leg, or shake a leg' originates from petty officers calling men to report for work. The women on board would simply show a leg to prove they were female, signalling that they were staying in the hammock and were not to be disturbed.

Visiting women were of course blamed by the Admirals for the spread of venereal disease among sailors, and officers had little sympathy regarding the degrading circumstances under which the women were forced to visit the ship. However, the principal reason for wives and other women visiting sailors on board ship was because it was the only way they could be sure to receive part of their partner's wages. For the women, and the sailors alike, the system that withheld the men's wages from their wives until their safe return was loathed and was the cause of much discontentment. This practice showed a lack of respect for sailors and their families, leaving women feeling humiliated because they could not be with their husbands or lovers in private. Nevertheless, it was imperative for women that they were rowed out to the ship when the paymaster was meeting the ship or they risked being left destitute over long periods of time.

An ordinary sailor's wages in the mid-nineteenth century was approximately 19 shillings a lunar month;[51] incredibly the same sum as paid a hundred years before, but still far more than the 15 shillings or so a month that our seamstress women residing ashore in sailortowns were earning. Sailor's pay at this time was less than that of a male labourer, who would earn approximately 30 shillings a month. A few pence were deducted from their wages for the sailors' Greenwich Hospital and for the Chatham Chest,

50   Cordingly D. *Heroines & Harlots. Women at Sea in the Great age of Sail.* Macmillan. 2001. p.259.
51   http://www.afamilystory.co.uk/history/wages-and-prices.aspx#Weekly-budget

being an early form of insurance.[52] Another fact was that most sailors would owe money to the ship's purser for clothing and tobacco, remembering that they may have been at sea for years.[53] Even when sailors' wives received some wages the money did not last for long. The women, separated for long stretches of time from their husbands, had to survive the best they could on shore.

Workhouses for Sailor Wives and Children

In sailortown, as in all towns, the Guardians of the Poor were accountable for issuing poor relief and had responsibility for managing the underfunded, overcrowded and miserable workhouses. Mothers, including sailor's wives, were separated from their children on entry into the workhouse and soon put to menial work. The first workhouse in Portsmouth was established in 1729, and by 1801 there were at least three more constructed in the region out of necessity. The new workhouses were built to accommodate aged and infirm seamen, local persons fallen on hard times, and orphan children. According to Suzanne Stark they were continually full with seamen's wives and their children, waiting to be transported back to their home parishes.[54] One option for the Guardians under the Act of Settlement and Removal was to transport paupers back to their parish of birth; under the Act the birth parish was responsible for a pauper's welfare. In Plymouth the Guardians of the Poor experienced the same problems as in Portsmouth. In 1758 the county was forced to bring in special legislation to raise extra funds to pay the costs of sending all the sailor families back to their home parishes.[55]

The problem of poverty amongst sailors' families was perennial. A century later in 1841, in Portsmouth, the Guardians were once again in dire financial straits because of the large number of destitute women and children living in the port. They outnumbered the men by nearly two to one, owing to so many sailors being away at sea. The 1841 census discloses that 2,881 males lived in Portsmouth, but an overwhelming 4,388 females resided in the town

---

52   The Chatham Chest was a fund set up in 1588 by the Royal Navy for disabled seamen, dockyard workers and their widows. In 1803, with an Act of Parliament the pension scheme was merged with the welfare schemes operated by Greenwich Hospital. After 1814 the physical Chests were removed from use and can now be viewed at the National Maritime Museum, London. Out of tradition sailors continued to refer to their welfare fund as the Chatham Chest.

53   Cordingly. op. cit. p.268.

54   Stark. op. cit. p.25.

55   Ibid. p.25.

too. David Cordingly writes that in some areas of the town many women had resorted to prostitution to support themselves. The Guardians of the Poor appealed to the Admiralty for financial aid as they could not provide relief for "the great numbers of Sailors and Soldiers, and their Wives and Families, and others, who Daily resort there".[56] Ironically, when women had word that their partner's ship had returned to port, they would often leave the workhouse and travel to greet their husbands. Then the revolving workhouse admission/removal process, and the risks associated with the harshness of the system, would start all over again.[57]

For women that were destitute, life on board ship could provide a sort of home, companionship, regular food and drink, travel, the possibility to explore new destinations, or even to leave sailortown for good. However, and most importantly, for low-paid women workers the higher wages paid to sailors must have been a financial incentive for potential women sailors. Naval personnel and those on other classes of maritime shipping would also receive prize money for capturing pirate or enemy ships when at war, the amount depending on rank.

56   Ibid. p.271.
57   For an excellent, in-depth examination of women and children in the workhouse, I refer the reader to Ball, Parkin, & Mills. *100 Fishponds Rd. Life and Death in a Victorian Workhouse.* Bristol Radical History Group. Pamphlet #34. 2015. Also, see Caldicott R. L., *The Life and Death of Hannah Wiltshire: A Case Study of Bedminster Union Workhouse and Victorian Social Attitudes on Epilepsy.* Bristol Radical Pamphleteer #35. 2nd ed. 2016. Also see Caldicott R . L. in Duffus J. *Women who Built Bristol 1184-2018.* Tangent Books. 2018. p.395.

Bristol Seaport: 1731

seven times with child
seven times the possibility
this woman's lottery:
once I gave birth –
two siren-eyed girls,
cold scarred, red-flushed,
watching the greasy sea blow
voyager's illicit dreams into the port.

you hear more than you understand
in this brazen sailor's town
where men come to make shameless alchemies.
I watch those storied armoured ships sail off to market: my girls' souls
lashed to the mast like lanterns.

so no more girls left; instead
two bleak women, emptied, indifferent.
tan or pale, no longer
clasped to the moment,
money's dream daughters
we sleepless in the narrow,
sea-damp cobbled street.

& somewhere in the south Atlantic,
after refusal of rum-soaked breath & left-overs,
a heavy sack hits the resistant water, flat,
dead of night, no moon or stars capable,
& the same soldiers who remember giving
my daughter's shabby, well-chewed coin
hitch up their pants and cough.

the loveliness is eaten by the sea.

—Elaine Savory[58]

58   Savory E. 'Bristol Seaport: 1731'. *Wasafiri*. Vol. 14. 1999. Is.28

A Few Known Black Women Sailors and the Slave Trade
(The Consequences of the African Slave Trade on Women)

To discuss trade between Africans and Europeans in the four centuries before colonial rule is virtually to discuss slave trade.

—Walter Rodney (1942-1980)

John Brown

John Brown was serving as a soldier-sailor marine on board the *Hannibal* in 1693, under Commander Thomas Phillips,[59] as a member of the Royal African Company's (RAC) private army.[60] John was discovered to be a woman by the ship's surgeon when a glister, a type of enema, was ordered by the ships' surgeon to be applied to her for relief from sickness.[61] Her illness in reality may have been a chronic gynaecological problem, perhaps miscarriage and not as perceived a rectal condition, the likely source of

---

59 For more information about Captain Thomas Phillips see Caldicott R.L. '*Should society memorialise a Slave Trader? The curious story of Brecon Town Council and the Plaque in honour of Captain Thomas Phillips, Slave Trader.*' https://www.brh.org.uk/site/articles/

60 The *Hannibal* began life as a huge wooden ship for its age, with a tonnage of 450 carrying 36 mounted guns. The guns would have been frequently used as they were against the French on 23 November, 1693.

The well connected Commander Phillips had found himself unemployed after his first ship was attacked by the French sailing back from Venice in 1689. Thomas Phillips became a part owner of the *Hannibal,* having a £10,000 investment in the Royal African Company ship. The then sub-governor of the RAC, Sir Jeffrey Jeffreys, was Phillips's patron and dispatched Phillips with the cash to buy the *Hannibal*. He and other merchants had a stake in the profits from carrying "elephants teeth, [tusks], gold, and Negro slaves, and having all meanful cargoes on board, where-with to purchase them, as well as supplies". (Phillips also carried Plain Cloth from Brecon as requested by the local African chiefs. Interview with Dr Ken Jones, July 2018). Phillips's brother was also on the voyage and died on the crossing to Africa on 27 January 1693. (See below Donnan. f.n. no.44. p. 394). On Phillips's belated return to Brecon he married and became Burgess of Brecon Town Council.

Phillips T. *A Journal of a Voyage made in the Hannibal of London, Ann. 1693, 1694, From England to Cape Monseradoe, in Africa, and thence along the Coast of Guiney to Whidaw, the Island of St. Thomas, and so forward to Barbadoes. With a Cursory Account of the Country, the People, their Manners, Forts, Trade, etc.* p. 3. Published by Churchill 1732, within a *Collection of Voyages and Travels. Vol.I.* http://play.google.com/books.

61 A medicine applied via the rectum.

bleeding in a man, or perhaps venereal disease. The ship was sailing at the time to one of the deplorable Gold Coast sailortown forts that held captive Africans for transportation to the West Indies. Also on board the *Hannibal* were other RAC soldiers and employees who were travelling as passengers.

John Brown (there is no other recorded name for her) had successfully enlisted in London as a male soldier for the RAC. The company specialised in running slave ships between West Africa and the West Indies, necessitating the RAC to carry their own soldiers on board to be stationed at the forts along the West African coast. On this voyage the vessel was carrying 30 soldiers directly employed by the RAC.[62] On Saturday, 18 November, 1693 Phillips remarkably recorded in his journal:[63]

> This morning we found out that one of the Royal African Company's soldiers, for their castles in Guiney [*forts in West Africa*] was a woman, who had entered herself into their service under the name of John Brown, without the least suspicion, and had been three months on board without any mistrust, lying always among the other passengers [*soldiers and envoys for RAC*] and being as handy and ready to do any work as any of them: and I believe she had contiu'd undiscover'd till our arrival in Africa, had not she fallen very sick, which occasion'd our Surgeon to visit her, and ordered her a glister, which when his mate went to administer, he was surpriz'd to find more sally-ports than can be expected, which occasion'd him to make a farther inquiry, which, as well as her confession, manifesting the truth of her sex, he came to acquaint me of it, whereupon, in charity, as well as in respect to her sex, I ordered her a private lodging apart from the men, and gave the tailor some ordinary stuffs to make her woman's cloaths; in recompence for which she prov'd very useful in washing my linin, and doing what else she could, till we deliver'd her with the rest [*passengers*] at Cape

62   Donnan E. '*Documents Illustrative of the History of the Slave Trade to America 1441-1700.*' Carnegie Institution of Washington Publication. No. 409. W. F. Roberts. vol.1. p.396. 1902.

63   The *Hannibal* became an English slaver (slave ship) operating the Trans-Atlantic slave trade. Over 700 enslaved Africans were forced into the slave decks. The individuals would not have been able to sit upright and were only allowed on the top deck in small numbers for an hour each day to exercise and take their food and drink.

Coast castle [*fort*].[64] She was about twenty years old and a likely[65] black girl.'[66] (Author's additions in italics).

The Commander did not appear to be overtly surprised to find a black woman soldier aboard his ship, and perhaps he did not record her true name because it might have been an obscure African name that he felt unimportant. Indeed, John Brown may not have been the only 'free' black soldier or sailor on board this or other slave ships. A study of passenger lists for RAC ships from 1694-1743 demonstrates that there were a small number of servants of the company classed as "Black" and "Mulatto" in the ledgers, including seamen and indigo workers. Roll calls of those employees present in RAC forts in West Africa in a similar period show that there were over a hundred soldiers of colour along with skilled workers including carpenters, bricklayers, gunsmiths, interpreters, hunters and fishermen.[67] So where did the RAC recruit black soldiers and servants, and where did they come from?

Established black communities have existed around the merchant ports of Britain for centuries, such as in Wapping in London, Toxteth in Liverpool and Butetown in Cardiff. It was from these sailortowns that young black men would be recruited as soldiers and seamen.[68] Amusingly, satirical writer Edward (Ned) Ward described the residents of Wapping as "salt water

64   Cape Coast Castle is one of around forty 'slave castles', or large commercial forts, built on the Gold Coast of West Africa, now Ghana. The fort was originally built by the Swedes for the trading of timber and gold, but went on to be used for the holding of enslaved people and gold in the trans-Atlantic slave trade. The castles are known as the "gate of no return" as the captives being shipped as slaves were to be sold in the Americas or Caribbean and would never return to their homelands. Cape Coast Castle was the RAC's strongest English fort along the coast. The government supported the maintaining of RAC forts, provided naval ships to defend the fort and gave the RAC access to its dockyards and stores. Paul J.H. 'The maintenance of British slaving forts in Africa: the activities of joint-stock companies and the Royal Navy'. http://www.unav.edu/documents. pp.6 to 7.

65   Another definition of the word 'likely' is attractive, as in a *likely* child. www.merriam-webster.com

66   Murdoch S. 'John Brown: A Black Female Soldier in the Royal African Company' *World History Connected* vol.1. no.2. p.1.

67   Find My Past *Britain, Royal African Company 1694-1743* https://search.findmypast.co.uk/search-world-Records/britain-royal-african-company-1694-1743-browse. It should be noted that designations of 'race' in the seventeenth and eighteenth century do not conform to modern day definitions.

68   For example, historian Ray Costello states that records between 1794 and 1805 show "76 free black sailors working on slave ships as being recruited in either Liverpool or their African or West Indian homelands." Costello, R. *Liverpool Black Community: The Early Years* Black History 365 Accessed 2018: https://www.blackhistorymonth.org.uk/article/section/real-stories/liverpool-black-community-early-years/

vagabonds". Writing in his satirical magazine, *London Spy*, during the late seventeenth century, Ward claimed:

> [Sailors] who are never at home but when they're at sea, and are always wondering when they're at home, and never contented but when they're on shore. They are never at ease till they're received their pay, and then never satisfied till they have spent it; and when their pockets are empty, they are just as much respected by their landladies (who cheat them of one half), if they spend the other.[69]

Wapping, as other sailortowns in the seventeenth and eighteenth centuries was a district that comprised the essential prerequisites for a transient nautical population: boarding houses, cheap inns, tailors, brothels, barbers, quack doctors, women with market stalls, small rowdy music halls; the venues for the requirements and entertainment of men. Magistrate John Fielding wrote of Wapping 'a man would be apt to suspect himself in another country. Their [the sailors] manner of living, speaking, acting, dress, and behaving are so peculiar to themselves.'[70] Could Fielding in fact be describing a multi-cultural space, when he writes that he "suspect himself in another country", giving reference to people of many ethnicities, languages and style of dress? There is good evidence to support this supposition. Estimates of the black population in the capital in the mid to late seventeenth century range from three to twenty thousand with many residents in the sailortowns of East London.[71] This would have been the London landscape that John Brown decided to leave behind; perhaps as a woman she felt that the ships moored on the Thames, and hence the seadog-life, was her only escape to make an independent living. It appears on the surface that Commander Phillips was respectful for John Brown's safety, being an RAC employee. He granted her privacy, giving her quarters away from the men once her true sex was discovered. She was given domestic work intended for women at the time, and dressed in female clothing specially ordered to be made for her. In comparison, another group of black nautical women were soon to be incarcerated on board the *Hannibal*. The lives of these women (and men) were to become a tragedy of unimaginable human horror. We know about the disaster that was about to unfold on the voyage to Barbados in 1694, because after the *Hannibal*

69   Edward (Ned) Ward (n.k.). *The London-spy; and vanities and vices of the town exposed to View (1667-1731)*. George H Doran Company, New York. p.243. University of Michigan. www.babel.hathitrust.org.
70   Quoted in Beavon. Ibid. p.1.
71   Olusoga, D. *Black and British: A Forgotten History* (London: Pan, 2017) pp. 85, 99-101, 161-164.

departed Ouidah (Whidaw) in West Africa the events were recorded in Phillips's journal.[72]. While laid over in the sailortown of Ouidah the RAC purchased a total of 1,300 enslaved Africans, with approximately one quarter being women. More than six hundred of the captives were destined to board the *East Indies Merchant* slaver that was to sail in convoy with the *Hannibal*. Commander Phillips writes in his Journal of 1693:

> Having bought my compliment of 700 slaves, viz. 480 men and 200 women, and finished all my business at Whidaw, I took my leave of the old king and his cappasheirs [*headmen*], and parted, with many affectionate expressions on both sides, being forced to promise him that I would return again the next year, with several things he desired me to bring from England; and having sign'd bills of lading to Mr. Pierson, for the negroes aboard, I set sail the 27th of July in the morning accompany'd with the *East India Merchant*, who had bought 650 slaves, for the island of St. Thomas, from which we took our departure, on August 25th, and set sail for Barbadoes.[73] We spent in our passage from St. Thomas to Barbadoes two months eleven days, from the 25th of August to the 4th of November following: in which time there happened such sickness and mortality among my poor men and Negroes. Of the first we buried 14, and of the last 320, which was a great detriment to our voyage, the Royal African Company losing ten pounds by every slave that died, and the owners of the ship ten pounds ten shillings, being the freight agreed on to be paid by the charter-party for every Negro delivered alive ashore to the African Company's agents at Barbadoes... The loss in all amounted to near 6500 pounds sterling. The distemper which my men as well as the blacks mostly died of was the white flux.[74]

72   Other spellings of Ouidah include Whidaw, Wydah and Whydaw. Ouidah was once known as the Kingdom of Whydah, apparently named after the Whydah Bird of Paradise. It is now an old African port (sailortown), located in modern Benin. Another explanation of the name is supplied by Paul J.H. 'Confusingly Ouidah takes its name from the Hueda (the tribal group), but was known locally as Glehue. Both Ouidah and Glehue have many valiant spellings, e.g. Whydah, Widah etc. op.cit. p.4
73   The St Thomas Phillips refers to is a small island off the west coast of Africa.
74   Phillips. *A Journal of a Voyage made in the Hannibal of London.* p.68. Ibid. Also, see Games A. and Rothman A. eds., *Major Problems in Atlantic History.* Houghton Mifflin. 2008. pp. 167-170.
White flux was a form of dysentery spread by insanitary living conditions.

The above passage in Phillips's journal states that he received 700 slaves on the *Hannibal*, however his gender break down only records 684 persons leaving a short-fall of 16 persons[75] This discrepancy may be obscuring the number of enslaved children, or people who were rapidly dying, as Phillips does mention that even before they left Africa the "cargo was dying at a rate of 3-4 a day". Another explanation may be that this is a typing error from the original hand written journal.

Table 1: Percentages of Slaves on board the *Hannibal* and mortality rates by gender and age 1663-1664 [76]

Number of slaves embarked	684 (700)*
Women	27%
Men	66%
Boys	6%
Girls	1%
Total males	72%
Total females	28%
Number of deaths in middle passage**	328
Mortality rate	47%

*700 on Trans-Atlantic Slave Trade Data Base. The figure of 684 is based on Phillips first set of journal figures.
** The middle passage refers to the sea journey undertaken by slave ships across the Atlantic..

Before boarding the *Hannibal* the male slaves were cuffed to one another in irons, and in pairs at their wrists and legs to prevent rebellion and to stop them attempting to jump overboard and escape. During the 'trading on boats' stage of rowing the Africans from the shore to the slave ship the RAC consortium would not have been covered by insurance to carry their human cargo, due to high rebellion and suicide rates. After all, unlike other commodities, Africans could resist. They would have only been covered for 'natural death'.[77] Phillips writes in his journal of how men who jumped overboard would be eaten by the many sharks that swam in the shallows.

75   Later in his journal Phillips writes he purchased 480 men and 220 women . Ibid. p. 62.
76   Phillips. op. cit.
77   Rupprecht A.' "Inherent Vice": Marine Insurance, Slave Ship Rebellion and the Law.' *Race & Class*. Sage Journals. Jan 18, 2018. p.6.

Females, males and children were branded on the chest with a small capital "H" to claim them for the *Hannibal*. According to Phillips the branding left a white mark and 'generally' healed up within 4 to 5 days because of their 'applying palm oil beforehand to smooth the wound'. This would effectively mean they were in fact frying human skin.

Three months later, when the ship arrived in Barbados, only 372 slaves remained alive on board. Horrifically 328 slaves had died while in transit, (based on the purchase of 700 people).[78] (See Table 1). Some had perished due to an outbreak of dysentery and smallpox while others had perished jumping overboard out of terror. It is alleged that some of the slaves, including women, were dumped overboard by the crew while still alive, as had happened previously on other slave ships. This murderous crime was committed in order that insurance claims– for loss of goods in transit–could be collected to assure a reprehensible trade was still profitable. The consortium of investors (the ship owners, the RAC, the captain and other shareholders), only received maritime insurance compensation for the slaves ('cargo') who died a 'natural death', excluding suicide, or in the circumstance of insurrection.[79] Phillips told an insurance inquiry: "We had about 12 negroes who did willfully *(sic)* drowned themselves" during the voyage whilst others persistently refused food, starving themselves to death.[80]

78   Author's note: There are a few discrepancies in the figures. There is a difference of 16 people as recorded in Captain Phillips's journal and the figures recorded on the *Trans-Atlantic Slave Data Base* that were sourced from documents held at The National Achieves, Kew, London. It may be that the discrepancies were: the children; or Phillips kept a few of the slaves to serve on him whilst at sea, or had purchased a few slaves to re-sale on privately in Barbados or elsewhere, as many captains were known to do; or to cover for deaths. However, the figures are representative of the massive involvement of the RAC mercantile interests in the slave trade.

79   On average an African male in his prime was insured for up to half to two thirds of his value at point of sale by the mid seventeenth century. Excess clauses were increasingly being added to policies throughout the eighteenth century by the insurers due to the high number of insurrections by captured Africans. Insurance cover was changed to 'not compensate for insurrection if less than five per cent, or sometimes ten per cent of the number of slaves held were killed.'"*Inherent Vice*": Marine Insurance, Slave Ship Rebellion and the Law'. Lobban M. 'Slavery, Insurance and the Law'. *The Journal of Legal History*. Vol. 28, 2007. Is. 3. p.1.

80   Murdock S. op. cit., p.4.

REPRESENTATION of an INSURRECTION
on board
A SLAVE-SHIP.

Shewing how the crew fire upon the unhappy Slaves from behind the BARRICADO, *erected on board all Slave ships, as a security whenever such commotions may happen.*

The text reads: Representation of an insurrection on board a slave-ship.
Showing how the crew fire upon the unhappy slaves from behind the
barricaddo, erected on board all slave ships as a security whenever such
commotions may happen.

Table 2: Chronological chart of the *Hannibal's* voyage (1693-1695). [81]

Departs London, Gravesend.	12 September 1693	70 Crew. Plus 30 RAC solders (one being John Brown, a woman) and 33 envoys, RAC Agents and passengers.* The *East Indies Merchant* sails with the *Hannibal*.
John Brown discovered to be a woman.	18 November 1693	Due to illness.
Hannibal damaged and involved in a sea battle.	23 November 1693	French incursion. (Capt. Phillips's brother mortally wounded).
Cape Verde islands for ship repairs.	27 Nov–6 Dec 1693	Captain Phillips taking opiates for head pains.
Hannibal reaches Guiney Coast.	23 December 1693	Travels down the coast with little luck in bartering goods on board for enslaved Africans.
Phillips's brother dies.	17 January 1694	From wounds sustained in the previous battle.
Whydah–Place of purchase of 1,300 slaves (African people) from the local African Chief.	21 May 1694	700 slaves picked up at Whydah, Bight (Bay) of Benin, Gulf of Guinea. John Brown disembarked from vessel.
Date departed West Africa.	27 July 1694	In convoy with the *East Indies Merchant*.
Called in at São Tomé (St. Thomas). A Portuguese colony off the West Coast of Africa.	11 August 1694 Departed 25 Aug	The *East Indies Merchant* stays behind in harbour for repairs.
Sails to Barbados.	Middle passage	Dysentery outbreak killing many slaves and crew.
Hannibal becalmed	4 October 1694	

81   Figures and dates taken from Phillips's Journal 1693-4. op. cit.

Hannibal arrives at Barbados.	4 November 1694	12 enslaved Africans died of smallpox on reaching Barbados. Only 372 slaves out of 700 disembark. 18 Crew die in Barbados.**
Hannibal departs Barbados for London.	3 May 1695	Phillips's journal states arrival in London during August 1695. (The later printed journal incorrectly records May 1694).

* Figure of 70 passengers cited on the Trans-Atlantic Slave Trade Data Base. 2013 Emory University. http://www.slavevoyages.org Accessed April 2018.
** Donnan E. *Documents Illustrative of the History of the Slave Trade*. op. cit. p.410.

Historian Roger Ball states that an African male in his prime between the years of 1680-1692, was valued on average at £18.73p per man. Women on the other hand were valued at 80 percent of this figure and a child at 50 percent.[82]

Phillips states in his journal that the Royal African Company lost ten pounds for every slave that died, and the owners of the ship ten pounds and ten shillings, being the freight agreed on to be paid by the charter-party for every Negro delivered alive ashore to the African Company's agents at Barbados. According to Phillips the loss in all amounted to nearly £6,500 pounds sterling, approximately £800,000.00 in today's value.

Phillips clearly differentiated the treatment of John Brown, the black female soldier, from the enslaved Africans held captive on board his ship. Interestingly Phillips states that while being entertained daily at the king's residence (the local chief), he enjoyed the food, entertainment and art, and he wrote about this extensively. This suggests that he recognised and appreciated a distinctive and elaborate culture, albeit based on a barter currency rather than coinage as he points out in his journal. So how did he justify his treatment of the hundreds of enslaved Africans he was about to cram into his ship? One reason might be that his 'cargo' were already enslaved, thereby sealing their fate, and in Phillips's eyes having been judged by 'their own'. Phillips in his journal does attempt to justify his own attitude to this incongruity. To rationalise his moral understanding of commanding a slaver Phillips differentiates between being of god's people, being Christian, and all Africans being barbarians and heathens, thereby implying that if they were

82   Ball R. 'Calculating the number of enslaved Africans transported by the Royal African Company during Edward Colston's involvement (1680-92)' Edward Colston Research paper #1 https://www.brh.org.uk/site/articles/edward-colston-research-paper-1/

not Christians they must be sub-human; a common intolerant racist theme made during this era and in modern times too.

> I who was born a PAGAN and a SLAVE
> Now sweetly sleep a CHRISTIAN in my GRAVE
> WHAT tho' my hue was dark, my SAVIOUR'S sight
> Shall change this darkness into radiant Light.[83]

In reality the true motive for the enslavement of Africans was not based on any kind of morality, religious or otherwise, but on rampant mercantile capitalism. The slave trade yielded high margins for elite merchants with further profits exacted from the exploitation of the labour of enslaved Africans in the Americas and the sale of slave produced commodities in Europe. African tribal leaders also profited by trading with Europeans. Phillips held a large personal financial investment in the first of these which undoubtedly provided his own personal motivation for his involvement in the 'vile trade'. According to comprehensive calculations by Behrendt and Hurley, captains who survived slaving voyages accumulated three times as much wealth as they would have earned in alternative maritime trades.[84]

We will probably never know the true motive for John Brown's ruse, but her decision to enlist as a soldier/sailor for the RAC raises questions such as: Did John know that she would be travelling on a slave trading ship when she enlisted; or just believed the *Hannibal* to be a merchant ship carrying cargo to trade in Africa? As we have already seen, the RAC employed a significant number of people of African descent as soldiers, sailors and skilled workers on the West African coast, some of whom were originally resident in London. This may have been because they would have had African language skills, some protection against sub-Saharan diseases, and in the hope they were more culturally acceptable when dealing with local slave traders in Africa.

The presence of African sailors on British merchant ships was not unknown in the eighteenth century, but what of the navy? A clue to this question can be found following the decision of Captain William Jones who had just assumed command of *HMS Goree* in 1761. Following several desertions and the deaths of most of the remaining crew from tropical diseases, including the previous captain, Jones needed crew quickly. Out of necessity he made the decision

83   Scipio Africanus, headstone effigy, Henbury Churchyard, Bristol. Servant to the Earl of Suffolk. Scipio died aged 18 in 1720. Cited in Dresser M. 2007. *Slavery Obscured. The Social History of the Slave Trade in Bristol.* Continuum. p.80.
84   Behrendt S.D., Hurley R.A. Liverpool as a trading port: Sailors' residences, African migrants, occupational change and probated wealth. *The International Journal of Maritime History.* Vol. 29 issue 4. pp. 875-910.

to take on a "black native" crew from Senegambia. These sailors would have had the added benefit of knowledge of the coastal and river routes along the coastline of West Africa. Interestingly one sailor on the list is named as Mary Sack, being the only female name amongst twelve African men. Mary offers us another fleeting example of a West African woman working on a British ship, this time in the Royal Navy.[85]

The records do not state when John Brown enlisted, or how many voyages she may have already undertaken, or even if this was in fact her first voyage as a soldier for the RAC. A plausible explanation as to why she signed up to a slaver may be the possibility that she was stealing her way back to the continent of her or her parent's birth; to find her family, homeland and culture. On the other hand she may have simply just wanted to live an independent life-style as a cross-dressing woman, being gender curious. Indeed, it must be considered that John was transgender, and wanted to live in the masculine interior space that a ship below decks comprised, and to work in a man's world among other male soldiers and sailors. In truth though, this option of employment might have been her way out of servitude and towards a level of financial independence–if she survived the voyage.

John was probably able to speak English, suggesting that she was probably born in London. She signed up with the RAC at a time when the company was recruiting large numbers of sailors and soldiers in London. She was a hard working spirited woman who had earned the respect and kindness of the crew. Phillips wrote "till we deliver'd her with the rest [*of the passengers*] at Fort Cape Coast castle", meaning that when the ship reached its destination she was to go ashore. Donnan, writes "The *Hannibal* landed 30 soldiers for the RAC, all in good health...though two months later nearly half had died".[86] From here on we do not know what became of the free black woman, John Brown. She may have been one of the soldiers who died in the Cape Coast castle, or perhaps her freedom was taken away once she lost her status as an RAC soldier. Paul writes of the RAC that 'difficulties of getting good building materials and skilled labour were compounded by problems of sickness and high mortality amongst Europeans.'[87]

The life of Commander Thomas Phillips has been memorialised with a slate plaque located where he lived. The plaque was erected in 2006 near to his former home (now St Ursuline Convent), at Captains Walk, Brecon, in Wales by Brecon Town Council. The placement of the £600 plaque proved

85   Foy C. R. 'The Royal Navy's employment of black mariners and maritime workers, 1754-1783'. *The International Journal of Maritime History*. 2016. Vol. 28. pp. 6-35.
86   Donnan. *Documents Illustrative of the History of the Slave Trade*. op. cit. p. 396.
87   Paul op.cit.7

very controversial at the time for the town council because it failed to mention that Phillips was a slaver and was directly responsible for the barbaric deaths of hundreds of captives. The plaque remains in place at the time of writing.

William Brown

Oh when I was a fair maid about seventeen
I enlisted in the Navy for to serve the Queen
I enlisted in the Navy, a sailor for to stand,
For to hear the cannons rattling, and the music so grand.
They sent me to bed, and they sent me to bunk.
To lie with the sailors, I never was afraid.
But putting off my blue coat, it often made me smile
To think I'd laid with a thousand men, and a maiden all the while.[88]

—Author Anonymous

The story of William Brown offers another remarkable account of a black female sailor. William had a successful naval career for at least twelve years on British warships, even serving as a captain of the foretop. Top-men were required to go aloft in all weathers to set or pull in the highest of sails. William would have led his seamen up the highest of masts and out along the yardarms, a hundred feet or more above the deck. The men would have to balance on nothing but a swaying rope and heave up or down the very heavy, often wet canvas sails; this task being the most dangerous role on the ship, other than firing the cannons. The following description of William Brown is taken from London's *Annual Register*, September 1815:

> She is a smart, well-formed figure, about five feet four inches in height, possessed of considerable strength and great activity; her features are rather handsome for a black, and she appears to be about 26 years of age. Her share of prize money is said to be considerable, respecting which she has been several times with the last few days at Somerset-Place. In her manner she exhibits all the traits of a British tar and takes her grog with her late messmates with the greatest gaiety.[89] She says she is a married woman, and

88   http://www.belgravehouse.com/online/excerpts/english_women_at_sea.html
89   1. Tar, also Jack Tar, slang for sailor. Sailors would often use tar to water proof their canvas clothing. *'Jack Tar: Myth and Reality. More than a List of Crew'*. Memorial University of Newfoundland 2011. www.mun.ca 2. Tar was also used to smooth hair in a sailor's pony-tail.

went to sea in consequence of a quarrel with her husband, who, it is said, has entered a caveat against her receiving her prize money. She declares her intention of again entering the service as a volunteer.[90]

William apparently joined the navy following a quarrel with her husband around 1804, and served on HMS *Queen Charlotte*, one of the largest ships in the fleet carrying 110 guns and with an enormous crew of 850 men. She obviously settled on board without any doubts concerning her gender from her fellow crewmen. If they did have any suspicions they must have kept them to themselves because the commander would have been informed immediately; instead he promoted her. Although discovered as a woman in 1815 (we do not know how, or her real name), she appears to have re-joined her ship later that year. A record in the ship's muster book refers to a 'William Brown, AB, entered 31 December, 1815, 1st Warrt., place of origin, Edinburgh, age 32.'[91] Some historians have argued that this could have been a different William Brown, but she did show up again in the summer of 1816, working aboard the HMS *Bombay*. William Brown's story is quite remarkable if nothing else for her nerve, courage and fortitude to be able to carry out her deception for so long while accomplishing a very physical and dangerous job.

Recruitment for the navy was a persistent burdensome problem for the British government during the eighteenth and early nineteenth century. An expanding empire and mercantile growth required a large, well trained and maintained navy. However, in certain geographical regions many white navy personnel were dying in large numbers from tropical diseases, particularly off the west coast of Africa. The British Navy was actively recruiting black seamen during the American Revolution by providing safe havens on board their ships between the years 1775-1777 for black runaway slaves. Charles Foy reveals in his article *The Royal Navy's employment of black mariners and maritime workers, 1775-1777*, some interesting facts about HMS *Rose*. He cites a 37 year old Guinea-born man named Tall Wheeler who became, along with other black men, 'friend[s] of the Government' after he boarded the *Rose* in November 1775. So, recorded as a 'friend', Wheeler began work on board as an Ordinary Seaman, but was then quickly promoted to Able Bodied Seaman. He died at sea, as many a sailor did, in October 1799. Furthermore, twenty-five black men

---

90   Baldwin, Cradock & Joy *the London Register or a View of the History, Politics, and Literature, for the year 1815*. London. 1824. p.64.
91   Cordingly D. *Women Sailors & Sailors' Women*. Random House. 2001. p.55.

served as sailors between 1775 and 1777 on the *Rose*.[92] The navy was able to provide, particularly during wartime, better working conditions for fugitive blacks, with some naval Officers occasionally assisting blacks to obtain their liberty once returning to port in England. However, as Foy correctly points out, the navy 'was not concerned in freedom for blacks but to keep its fleet at sea.'[93] This may have been the fate of some unknown black women too, who disguised themselves as male sailors to escape to England.

Another interesting fact is that with many British ships ever present in the West Indies during the mid-eighteenth century the press gangers would take advantage of roaming 'masterless' blacks and impress them into the British Navy. Admiral Colvill described impressed black sailors as having 'shared the same Fate with such freeborn [as] White Men, as we could pick up'.[94] Royal Navy press gangs were also robustly active around and in the small ports either side of Massachusetts before the outbreak of the War of Independence.

England at this time had no judicial consensus as to whether black people were in fact free once landed in England. But in 1792 Lord Mansfield decreed, regarding black rights, that slavery was 'so odious that nothing can be suffered to support it [in England] but positive law'. This became known as the Somerset Decree. However, the Somerset decision did not decree that slavery was actually illegal in England, thereby leaving the legality issue open to debate. Unwittingly though, many blacks believed that the decree did in fact 'emancipate' them from slave status upon reaching the shores of England. This understanding, combined with the British military welcoming runaways into its ranks during the American Revolution, led to several thousand former slaves reaching England, many being mariners. The freedom black mariners found in England was limited; they remained subject to re-enslavement, had limited legal protections over employment conditions and were often homeless and poor, as being the condition of pauper working class British people at the time. Despite such conditions, 'life in England was a considerable improvement over enslavement in the Americas for many former slave mariners.'[95]

Through extensive research of *The Black Mariner Database* (BMD), Foy established that in 1775 there were no less than 1,300 identified black naval crew listed, one being a Captain John Perkins commanding the

92   Foy. op. cit.
93   Foy. op. cit. p.9.
94   TNA, ADM 1/482, Alexander Colvill to the Admiralty, Spithead, 29 October 1762. Cited in Foy op. cit. p.11
95   Foy C. R. 'Unkle Sommerset's' freedom: liberty in England for black sailors'. *Journal for Maritime Research*. vol.13. no.1. 2011. pp. 21-36. Published online 9 May 2011.

Punch 1778-1779. However, he was the absolute exception, being the only black man to have commanded a merchant ship at this time.[96] According to Stark, the *Annual Register* of 1815-1864 names a number of black naval crew, including slaves sent to sea by their masters, and it appears that despite racial discrimination on the land blacks were welcome on board ship.[97]

Free black men working as sailors were commonplace on slave ships, according to W. Jeffrey Bolster.[98] Black people were able to spread news, gossip, greetings and friendships around the slaving coast of West Africa–between the enslaved and pseudo-free blacks. Words of revolts and news from across the waters were also being carried between the communities of the Americas and Europe. Black sailors in the era of slavery and "fellow countrymen", shaped seafarers' communities that were distinctively black wherever their vessels docked, at home in London and across to the West Indies.[99] Black sailors would work on the slave ships as cooks, officers' servants and occasionally as pilots and among the black enslaved cargo where their role might be to serve food and guard the slaves. Only very rarely would a black sailor be promoted, making William Brown's career even more remarkable and virtually unique as far as the records exist.

Mortality Rates of Crew on Slave Ships

Working on a slave ship was not a popular choice for sailors, who suffered high rates of mortality due to dreadful working conditions and the hardships experienced working in the tropics. The RAC had problems recruiting sailors due to high death rates, and also due to the immorality of the trade. A study of crew mortality was carried out between 1780 and 1807 by Stephen D. Behrendt. He has examined 1,709 muster rolls for Liverpool slave voyages and discovered that 17.8 percent of the original crew died, 10,439 out of 58,778. He believed that 11% of the men died of fevers like malaria contracted on the West Coast of Africa, and of dysentery and similar gastrointestinal diseases.[100] However, surprisingly, or not so surprisingly, as most sailors could not swim, a large number of men had also died from drowning. Sailors who were sick on arrival at their destination would be left behind, without pay, to receive treatment so as not

96   Ibid. p.15.
97   Stark. op. cit. p.185.
98   Bolster W. J. *Black Jacks: African American Seamen in the Age of Sail*. Harvard University Press. 1997.
99   Ibid.
100   Behrendt S.D., Hurley R.A. op.cit.

to contaminate the remaining crew. The policy was that sailors could only receive their pay at the end of a completed voyage back in England, albeit that the slavers actually made three separate voyages. The implications for their families were dire.

Mortality rates and crew conditions on slavers were critical too for the women of sailortowns left behind. Mark Steeds, in *Cry Freedom Cry Seven Stars,* his work about the abolitionist Thomas Clarkson in Bristol during 1787, cites Clarkson: '...just like their counterparts in the Navy, slave ship owners used any means available to recruit sailors aboard their vessels. Getting their victims blind drunk, in debt or by just cracking them over the head, was all fair game to these ruthless individuals...of 940 men who served on Bristol slave ships in 1786, 239 deserted and 216 died at sea.'[101] This puts the total number of crew lost from the ships at 455 or 48.4 %, about half of the crew in just one year alone. The average loss of crew on a slave voyage stood at about 23%, the same average mortality rate as for slaves dying on a typical voyage. The consequences of the African slave trade were to be felt in many sailortown homes around the world.

Women were deeply affected in many ways by the slave trade. Firstly, the enslaved African women, torn from their homelands by black slavers, shackled and marched across the vastness of Africa to be held in African sailortown forts and then holed up in ships like the *Hannibal*. Secondly, the sailors' wives of the crews upon slaving ships who risked losing their lives because the work was so dangerous and with a far higher risk of dying from disease. Thirdly, the black women sailors and soldiers, travelling for personal reasons unknown, disguised as men. Fourthly, the wealthy women who were part of the elite merchant class, sometimes actively engaged in the procurement of African slaves, including child slaves from Africa. Finally not forgetting the female abolitionists, but that is another story.

---

101   Steeds M. *Cry Freedom Cry Seven Stars.* op. cit. pp.10-11.

Impressment—Protagonist Women!
(Resistance, Opposition and the Struggle to Survive)

Of all the anomalies that have probed a reproach to the British constitution and an inherent cause of gangrene and disorder, the pressgang appears to have been the most odious in its origin and the least excusable for its results.

—William Johnson, 1842

Many voyages were months or even years in duration. Mariners encountered stormy seas, pirate attacks, privateer raids, mutinous revolts, floggings, incurable diseases, accidents aboard ship. But worse of all they feared meeting a roaming press gang. The women left behind after press gangers had stolen their men away were also victims of the hated involuntary method of recruitment employed by the Royal Navy, known as impressment.

Thousands of women and children were left ashore having no idea how they were to survive without the regular income earned by the men in the community, prompting women to write letters to the Admiralty petitioning for the return of their husbands and sons. (The men were only paid a lump sum upon their return to port, if they returned at all). In his seminal work *The Evil Necessity*, Denver Brunsman refers to these women as 'impressment widows' and cites an example of the effects of this practice. In Tyneside, located in the North East of England, in the 1770s, poor relief had trebled due to the multitude of missing wage-earners who had been seized by press gangs, resulting in many families becoming destitute.[102]

Impressment was a legal and organised system employing notorious gangs of thugs to forcibly seize men to serve in the Royal Navy.[103] The Crown claimed a permanent right to capture men for the navy, supported by parliament. In times of war, particularly the French Wars, the numbers of impressed men would rise dramatically. In the seventeenth and eighteenth centuries at least a third to a half of Royal Navy personnel were pressed, leading to tens of thousands of men being kidnapped by the British state.[104] During the conflicts with France between 1793 and 1815 the impressment service operated in all British coastal towns and ports. Although mainly

102   Brunsman D. *The Evil Necessity: British Naval Impressment in the Eighteenth-Century Atlantic World*. University of Virginia Press. 2013.
103   Impressment was employed since the early medieval period and continued up until after the Napoleonic Wars.
104   Hochschild, A. *Bury the Chains. The British Struggle to Abolish Slavery* (London: Pan, 2005) pp.222-223.

The text on the banners reads:
"Wilkes, Liberty and Hallifax for ever" and "down with all Liberty Sandwich for ever."

The Press Gang, 1770. Women and children cry and plead as an artisan,
wearing an apron, is taken by a press gang.

seeking out former sailors, merchant sailors and fishermen, magistrates also granted powers for the service to press able-bodied unemployed men, who had never been to sea before, known as landsmen. Boys and young men in workhouses could also be 'apprenticed' to sea under the vagrancy laws, and able bodied mariners who were in the workhouse could, and were, impressed against their will.[105]

The government department responsible for this particular iniquitous arrangement for drafting naval seaman was known as the Impress Service. Armed with pistols and clubs the 'gangers' went about seizing men aged between eighteen to fifty-five to serve on British warships for up to five years. Press gangs were legitimate armed naval squads of ordinary seamen, led by naval officers. The officers who led the press gangs were strangely named as 'the rendezvous'. Sailortowns would be specifically targeted, being places inhabited by merchant seamen, fishermen, sea pilots and shipwrights. They were also the obvious locations where men would be socialising and drinking, staying in boarding houses, or living with their families while on shore leave or having left the navy.

Historian Nicholas Rogers has quantified impressment. He concludes that of the 450,000 men that served in the British Navy between 1740 and 1815, 40% were pressed, in other words nearly half of all naval crew were forced against their will into military service during the time.[106] Denver Brunsman calculates a similar figure, estimating that perhaps a quarter of a million men were pressed into the navy, being the largest group of forced labourers after African slaves in the British Empire.[107] We do not know precisely how many wives and mothers were dependent on the pressed men's regular wages but it would have been a very high number.

Britain had a huge merchant navy due to the nation's maritime trading empire and that meant an enormous number of high quality professional merchant sailors were required. It is estimated that in 1812 Britain had 120,000 men (and a few unknown women), serving in the merchant navy. The irony is that in war time the merchant ships were even more important than in peace time. Merchant ships kept supplies coming in and acted as troop ships. However, this did not stop sailors in the merchant fleet from being pressed into the Royal Navy. The tactic operated by press gangs was to board a merchant ship before the vessel had returned to port and moored up, The strategy was

---

105   Workhouse Admission Books in port regions reveal many sick and elderly mariners as residing in the workhouses.

106   Rogers N. *The Press Gang. Naval Impressment and its opponents in Georgian Britain.* Bloomsbury. 2009. p.40.

107   Brunsman D. *The Evil Necessity.* op. cit.

deliberate as it allowed the captain and remaining crew left on board to off-load the cargo, albeit with a reduced crew, therefore not disadvantaging merchants' profits. The unfortunate sailors who were given over to the press gangs were at the mercy of the captain to give them their end of voyage pay off, with many being under-paid. At the same time, in response to naval impressment powers, some merchant ships had special hiding places built into the ships to conceal sailors when being approached by suspected press gang vessels.

Nicholas Rogers writes that the old vagrancy laws, with coercive use of impressment, were designed to keep males from entering the workhouse. It was considered "the masterless men and women who had to be compelled to labour, whose social irregularity was a moral affront to discipline and subordination".[108] In other words, the rectification of a perceived lack of moral discipline in some working class men could somehow justify the act of forcibly pressing them into the navy. Also, for the workhouse Guardians and on behalf of local authorities, the Admiralty might at times compensate the rate payer, thereby in theory lowering the rate of workhouse admissions during times of failed harvests and economic depression. At the same time, in the background, wives, family and friends would be eagerly waiting for the returning ship to moor up and the sailors on board would be looking forward to receiving their hard earned wages and what every sailor yearns for—shore leave, if permitted.

There are many descriptive accounts recorded about the men who were forcibly impressed, but very few primary or secondary sources re-calling women's reaction to the impressment service. As a consequence, representations of women impacted by impressment have rarely survived. On a depressing note there are a few shocking records of women being hanged after their sailor husbands were stolen away; executed for petty thieving, such as stealing pieces of cloth to sell for food to feed their children. It is indisputable that the women left impoverished due to impressment suffered as much as the pressed men, but at least the men had ships' rations and shelter of sorts. It should be noted that if an impressed man deserted back to his family, or another ship, and was caught, the penalty was extremely brutal, two to four hundred lashes or even hanging in some cases.

Rogers is foremost among nautical historians in having researched impressment in relation to the expansion of republican revolutionary philosophy that was growing in both Europe and the Americas during the eighteenth century. He compares the number of anti-impressment riots in England with food and labour disturbances, thereby posing the theory that

108   Rogers N. 'Vagrancy, impressment and the regulation of labour in eighteenth-century Britain'. *Slavery and Abolition.* vol. 15. is.2. pp.102-113. Published on line 13 Jun. 2008.

the labouring poor both on land and at sea were united in a sense of a total disconnect with the elite classes.[109]

Food/grain riots:	900+	for 1740-1801
Impressment riots and affrays:	602	for 1738-1805
Violent labour disputes:	383	for 1717-1800

It is probable that numerous local skirmishes over food and wages with the landed gentry were never reported unless the local militia were called out. Localised resistance to press gangs, for example in taverns, on the quayside, on board ship, or on farmland, tended not to be included in the official records. Therefore it is highly likely that the quantified number of anti-impressment riots and affrays would have been rather higher than the records suggest.

By the eighteenth century a powerful, well-armed and fully crewed navy was fundamental to the defence and expansion of the British Empire, and to maintain commerce around the globe. The Royal Navy was crucial for the protection of merchant interests between continents, colonies and British ports in the United Kingdom. Maintaining the movement of goods and people (including the enslaved) was paramount, and served the interests of a rapidly growing elite class of merchants. By the mid eighteenth century Britain had become the wealthiest merchant and ship owning nation in the world. The Merchant Navy was protected by the Royal Navy, and yet sailors were being impressed from merchant naval crews, resulting in a growing tension between the Admiralty and merchant ship owners on both sides of the Atlantic. Despite a conflict of words between the two naval brands, the policy provoked a further incursion into the lack of rights for sailors when the threat of impressment began to be sanctioned as a form of punishment on prospective mutineers serving on merchant ships.

Sailors were increasingly objecting and challenging the authority of senior officers due to the harsh conditions and their treatment on board ship. Radical philosophies regarding concepts such as republicanism, liberty and freedom in response to exploitative colonial capitalism and an autocratic top down leadership were now being circulated orally from ship to ship. Republicanism and the Rights of Man (human rights), were paramount in the mind of an impressed sailor from the 'New World'; perhaps too for the women left behind.

Christopher Magra puts forth a robust argument that sailors' revolutionary thoughts were instrumental in accelerating the American War of Independence, also known as the American Revolutionary War (1775-

109 Rogers N. *Press Gang.* op. cit. p.39.

57

1783).[110] Naval and merchant crews were international, with some ships being crewed by sailors from over ten different countries. Men were impressed and signed up from across the world, including Europe, Asia, the Americas and Africa. Peter Linebaugh and Marcus Rediker expand on the premise:

> This was a 'shared experience' of capitalist expropriation and exploitation, that linked merchant mariners, pirates, slaves, and those involved in anti-impressment collective actions on a transatlantic, man-headed proletariat that resisted Herculean efforts on the part of a ruling class to keep workers in check.[111]

The shared radicalism against state sponsored forced labour was embraced in an 'anti-impressment collective' by both men and women. Resistance was coming from bottom up—below deck, also from distressed women in sailortowns, and from revolutionary statesmen such as Benjamin Franklin. Leaders of early socialist movements in England such as feminist Mary Wollstonecraft argued in 'A Vindication of the Rights of Woman' that 'impressment was a women's issue'.

For any man, suddenly taken from their home and occupation, to be dragged on board a ship, a man-of-war, to risk his life, limbs, sight, sanity and liberty without a moment's notice, was thoroughly reprehensible—a practice of unjustified state-sanctioned kidnapping. Public opinion achieved significant resistance to impressment with many believing the system an outrage, particularly in sailortowns. Even more so in that the men were not even entitled to an advancement of pay to equip themselves with a few necessaries before sailing, such as a hammock and clothing. They relied instead on their women folk delivering provisions to their place of confinement, the women often having to pay to be rowed out to the tenders and ships where the men were being held. Later this indignity, among others, was to be challenged as one of the key demands of the sailor delegates at the Nore Munity of 1797.

Press gangs often met their nemesis in the form of the women of sailortowns. Below are some examples of resistance, often violent, that were meted out to the press gangs by local people. Sailortown women were instrumental in instigating resistance to impressment through riots and protests. There are

110   Magra C. 'Anti-Impressment Riots and the Origins of the Age of Revolution, Mutiny and Maritime Radicalism in the Age of Revolution: A Global Survey'. *International review of social history*. Special Issue 21.. 2013. pp.131-151
111   Linebaugh P. and Rediker M. *The Many-Headed Hydra. Sailors, Slaves, Commoners, and the Hidden History of the Revolutionary Atlantic*. Beacon Press, Boston. 2000. p.329.

The Liberty of the Subject by James Gillray. 1779. Women try and prevent the impressment of a tailor.

accounts of women raising the alarm as their men were snatched away, often evoking a mob to violently attack the press gangers. It is known that sailors often took jobs on inland farms or navvy jobs like building canals, to evade impressment. A marvellous comical image is drawn up when in Barking, Essex a press gang seized some former sailors and were then set upon by 'a numerous body of Irish hay-makers, armed with sabres and pitchforks…'[112]

Press gangs were also very active in the West of England, particularly in the region of Bristol and Gloucester. On 9 May 1759 Lieutenant McKinley, commanding officer of a press gang, dropped anchor at King Road, near the village of Pill, a small sailortown situated on the River Avon at the mouth of the Severn Estuary, roughly five miles from the Port of Bristol. Pill was the base for most of the pilots aiding ships to pass through the fast and high tidal reaches of the Severn Estuary and along the Avon Gorge into Bristol. The Pill Pilots were vital to sustain merchant shipping on this notoriously dangerous waterway full of sand and mud banks. McKinley, a drunkard, and the captain decided to go ashore, leaving the pressed men on board locked in down below. Surprisingly, according to accounts at the time, a few of the

112   Land I. *'Domesticating the Empire: Culture, Masculinity and Empire in Britain, 1770-1820'* PhD. Dissertation. University of Michigan, 1999.

pressed men's wives were on board the boat too, and whilst the officers were on shore getting drunk, using an axe and hatchet no less, they managed to hack through the chains that bound the men. Fourteen of the 20 men fled, taking all the guns and a boat, never to be found by the authorities.[113]

Another incident took place on the night of 16 October 1778. Anne Jenkins and her husband Charles were asleep in bed at their river side home in Blakeney, a village that lies close to the Forest of Dean along the Severn Estuary near Gloucester, north of Bristol. Anne was woken in the middle of the night by the sound of the front door being forced. Running downstairs, grabbing a pick to defend herself, she opened her front door to see men in rough blue uniforms–it was the press gang and they were about to steal her husband away. The *Gloucester Journal* reported the story:

> She had scarcely taken her post there before six fellows broke into the house and the foremost presented himself at the foot of the stairs with a loaded pistol, swearing he would have her husband, and attempting to come up, the woman told him she would stick the pick thro' him if he came any further, the fellow persisted and as he came near the top of the stairs she stuck the pick into him. He fell and dropt his pistol upon the stairs, which she instantly swept down and caught, and gave to her husband who stood behind her at the top of the stairs, and bid him defend himself. The five other men seeing their comrade fall by the hands of a woman, were exasperated and attempted to rush up the stairs, but the woman still maintained her post and as the foremost advanced she struck the pick quite thro' his temples: this man's fate threw such a damp upon his comrades that they instantly retreated.

Charles Jenkins had been targeted by a press gang because he was an experienced sailor, as many men in the region were. According to John Powell's research the injured press gang leader, known as John Young, died three days later from his injuries and was buried the next day in Awre churchyard.[114] Anne was committed to Gloucester's Castle Gaol on a charge of murder. A report was uncovered by Powell, which reads:

> Criminal as this woman may appear at present in the eye of the law, there is great reason to hope that when the fatal act shall be

113   Rogers N. op.cit.
114   Powell J. 'Press Gang Violently Thwarted at Blakeney'. *Forest of Dean Local History Society*. Aug. 2017.

fully investigated it will be found to have proceeded not with malice aforethought but with a sudden irresistible impulse of conjugal affection… She is now big with child and was committed with an infant in her arms who she supports in prison. It ought not to be omitted that the wretchedness of a gaol at this severe season is aggravated by her having offered to surrender herself for trial at the last Assize when she could not be arraigned on account of her not having observed the forms necessary on such occasions. Any donations will be received and applied to the woman's use by the Rev B Newton.

There later appears a report in the *Calendar of the Criminal Prisoners in the Castle Gaol of Gloucestershire at the Trinity Sessions*, 11 July, 1780:

Ann Jenkins 'Brought in January 8, 1780, committed by 13, Newton, Clerk, to answer to a Bill of Indictment presented to the Grand Inquest and found true against her for the wilful murder of John Young—Out on bail'

Powell writes that it would appear that Ann Jenkins was released on her charge of murder because local officials had no sympathy for the immoral jurisdiction of press gangs. The fact that she had been pregnant, and with a young child held with her in gaol in the cold of winter, appears to have been a consideration too. Gloucester Castle Gaol, where Ann was held awaiting her court appearance, was ironically the same county goal and place of detention for those who had been impressed. Apparently pressed men could gain their freedom for a price, as one report refers to the keeper there, Richard Evans, possessing a magic palm… "rub it with silver in sufficient quantity and the 'street door to the gaol' opened before you…"[115]

Yet another press gang met with furious opposition when encountering the women of Pill. During the night of 1805 a press gang was active in the village looking for men to steal for the navy. A Lieutenant McKenzie, leader of a press gang, entered a pub run by Joseph Hook. He attempted to impress a seaman and was attacked by Mrs Hook, her daughter, and a female servant. McKenzie complained that he had been violently assaulted by the women, who had torn his uniform and that Joseph Hook had made no attempt to prevent the attack. Due to intelligence reports, the Pill pilots were known by the Admiralty to be offloading sailors before reaching the Port of Bristol: far west on the Severn Estuary in the many smaller harbours along the coast such

115   Powell, op. cit.

as Ilfracombe in Devon. If the pilots were challenged or seized by Admiralty Officers the Merchant Venturers of Bristol would soon secure their release in order to keep goods moving in and out of the Port of Bristol.[116]

In Bristol there was violent collective opposition to the press gangs with many sailors fighting back. Every single member of a press gang operating for a few months in Bristol during 1759 had been badly injured and one was even killed.[117] Women of Bristol who had suffered their husbands snatched away by press gangs wrote to the Admiralty to complain and plead that the men be sent home to support their families. Records reveal three such cases, Mary Jacobs, Lucy Castle and Mary Creed. Needless to say their objections to the men being pressed into the Royal Navy were turned down. Mary Creed was pregnant in 1806 and living in lodgings at Mrs James houses in Griffin Lane, Bristol, when her husband, a former ships' steward, was seized by a press gang.[118] She wrote the following letter to the Secretary of the Admiralty:

Sir, You will be pleased to lay before the Lords Commissioners of the Admiralty the deplorable situation I am in by having my husband, who is very sickly and unfit for the service, taken from me by the Press gang here. I am big with child, and have no other way of support but him, he likewise supporting his old father and mother, and if he was examined by any Doctor he would be found more fit for a hospital than a ship, having entirely lost the use of his right hand.[119]

Her plea was turned down.

During 1811 in the City of Hull it was reported that three or possibly four local men were working as members of a press gang. They were paid 10 shillings for every man they captured and because they were local they had the advantage that they knew where sailors on shore leave would be lodged. One of the local men was Jem White who was once himself a local seaman. One night Jem's home was attacked "by a crowd, principally women, vowing his destruction". He had to resort to defending himself with a cutlass until he was rescued by a party of soldiers and ironically was taken to a pressing tender (holding boat), for his own protection.[120]

116   Poole S. op.cit. p.66.
117   Hochschild A. *Bury the Chains*. op. cit. p.224.
118   Today Griffin Lane is part of Lower Park Street, Bristol, close to the docks.
119   Spavens W. op. cit. *Memoirs of a Seafaring Life. The Narrative of William Spavens. Pensioner on the Naval Chest at Chatham.*
120   Lavery B. *Royal Tars. The Lower Deck of the ROYAL NAVY 875-1850* Conway p.207. 2010.

William Spavens, originally himself a pressed sailor, wrote in his *Memoirs of a Seafaring Life* about the time when he was part of a press gang of 20 men led by an officer operating on Dublin Bay.[121]

> When we perceived a ship coming in, we concealed ourselves, and let only the wherry men be seen, who were pilots...one day as the *Dubliner* Letter of Marque[122] from New York was coming in, we sheered under her lee, asking if they wanted a pilot? The Captain said they did, and told us to come along side; but the men having some suspicion of our design, bid us keep off, or they would fire upon us... ...Having no chance of succeeding by daylight we sent for re-enforcements from Dublin and during that night the press gang attempted again to steal away the sailors but unexpectedly came across a woman and child on board.

Spavens' account makes for enthralling reading:

> [We] boarded...but finding the men had taken close quarters, we scuttled their decks with axes, and fired down amongst them, while they kept firing up at us where they saw the light appear. After having shot one of our men through the head, and another through both his thighs, they submitted, and we got 16 brave fellows. There was a woman and a child in a side cabin in the state room, neither of which had received any injury, although the ceiling above them was full of shot-holes...

> Such are the methods frequently made use of to obtain seamen for the service in this land of liberty. It seems shocking to the feelings of humanity, for a sailor, after he has been a long voyage, endured innumerable hardships, and is just returning to his native land with the pleasing hope of shortly beholding a beloved wife and children, some kind of relations, or respected friends, to be forced away to fight, perhaps to fall, and no more enjoy those dear connextions—it is a hardship with nothing but absolute necessity can reconcile to our boasted freedom.[123]

---

121   Spavens. op. cit. p.46.
122   The Letter of Marque: 1. A document permitting a privateer to operate. 2. A merchant ship on a trading voyage, but having a letter of marque in order to profit by any chance of capturing another ship.
123   Spavens. op. cit. p.46.

Women were involved and sometimes injured in collective attempts to prevent men being pressed. Spavens recounts how his crew of press gangs were (reluctantly) put ashore in Liverpool docks in an attempt to capture sailors for the navy. They succeeded in seizing 16 men but only one was a sailor so the other 15 were released. However, the next day with the press gang comprising of 80 men they were able to surprise the crew of the *Lion* while they were in the customs house renewing their protections.[124] Seventeen men were captured and held, being guarded out on the street. The local people heard of what was taking place and Spavens recalled:

> several hundreds of old men, women, and boys, flocked after us, well provided with stones and brickbats, and commenced a general attack; but not wishing to hurt them, we fired our pistols over their heads, in order to deter them from further outrage; but the women proved very daring, and followed us down to low water mark, being almost up to the knees in mud.[125]

The description clearly demonstrates that women were proactive in taking part in 'riots' with other members of the community in order to protect the men from being impressed. The extraordinary, former cross-dressing woman sailor and soldier Hannah Snell, who we met in the last chapter, was the married landlady of the *Three Tuns* public house in Southwark. Hannah was a woman to be reckoned with. In 1771, after witnessing the kidnapping of a suspected sailor by a press gang, she accosted the Lieutenant in charge. On her demanding the captive be released "he refused and with bad words ensuing, she grabbed hold of him and shook him. Two sailors stepped forward to rescue the officer." Apparently Hannah then challenged the rest of the gang to a stick or fist fight. Her only proviso was that she be permitted to pull off her stays, gown and petticoats and to put on a pair of breeches. She shouted that "she had sailed more leagues than any of them, and if they were seamen, they ought to be on board, and not sneaking about as kidnappers", she continued "but if you are afraid of the sea, take Brown Bess on your shoulders, and march through Germany as I have done: Ye Dogs, I have more wounds about me than you have fingers. This is no false attack; I will have my man". The sailor backed off and Hannah took the distressed man to his home to be looked after by his grateful wife.[126]

124 A document granting exemption from impressment.
125 Ibid. p.48
126 Major. J. *Hannah Snell: The Amazons and the Press Gang, 1771. All Things Georgian.* www.georgianera.wordpress.com

Were women sailors ever discovered on board ships or in the ports during press gang raids? Undoubtedly there were a few, some who served as men in the merchant navy undetected, retaining their disguise, but there were others who resisted impressment by exposing their gender. Hannah Whitney's career in the merchant navy was cut short when she was snatched by a press gang in Plymouth during 1761. Dressed in male sailor clothing she, along with the other male victims, was placed in the town prison so they could not escape. Realising the horror of her predicament, she apparently had a claustrophobic attack while in prison which led her to confess to being female. Hannah told the authorities that she had been aboard British warships for over five years. She was promptly released, but what happened to her after her release is not known. Perhaps she re-enlisted at a later date, changing her name once again as some women might have done.

"The press gang was merely the first step to the barbarities [of] the British Royal Navy." So wrote William Johnson in 1842. Johnson correctly believed that the fleets were being manned by a "force of relentless cruelty"[the officer class], with "unhappy wretches"[the working class], "imprisoned on board who were treated in a way better befitting to condemned felons, impressment being such an awful punishment for no crime committed." In other words, that innocent men were being impressed onto floating, stinking hulks and living in worse and more dangerous conditions than convicted criminals.

> From the hour he became an involuntary seaman he was too often cut off from all communication with friend or relative, and generally sent to an unhealthy climate. Here predisposed to disease from the sudden transition, life was either lost or rendered merely a burden for the future; exposed to a duty harassing in the extreme, he was placed under the absolute disposal of a petty monarch, whose slightest caprice was indisputable law; yet under all there oppressive afflictions he possessed no appeal from any wrong, save to a code of jurisprudence so severe, that every line appears to have been traced in blood, and every other penalty is a shameful death. This then was the moral condition of the impressed seamen.[127]

Impressment was finally ended after the defeat of Napoleon in 1814 due to the Royal Navy substantially reducing the size of the fleet.

127   Neale, Johnson W. (also William Johnson). *History of the Mutiny at Spithead and the Nore; with an Enquiry into its Origin and Treatment: and Suggestions for the Prevention of Future Discontent in the Royal Navy.* London: T. Tegg. 1842. p.B.2

Pecked by the seagulls
Hanging from the gallows
Swinging in the breeze
Dripping something on the streets
I can see him from my window
They can see him from the water
Just a victim of the press gang
I knew him when he was breathing
He was a good man
He was a young man
He was like you, he was like me.
It could've been me
It could've been me.
Twisting in the breeze
(Cut him down, cut him down)
Left for the children on the street
On the street.
He should've kept his mouth shut
He never shoulda
Left that ship
Don't go drinking
Down by the docks
You don't know
If you'll wake up.
Woke up on the water
No one ever asked him if he wanted
To go
Didn't have many options,
He was smart. He got out
When he could
Should've stayed in the Pacific
Could have had it good...
Should've been the press gang
Should've been the press gang
Cut him down. [128]

---

128   The Murder City Devils. *'Press Gang'. 'In Name and Blood.'* Track list released 2000.
Also, on live album *R.I.P.* 2003. Worth a listen to live recording at http://www.youtube.com.
The composition brings out the horror of running away from ship after impressment.

Part Two

'Romance of the Sea'

Put on a jolly sailor's dress
And daubed her hands with tar,
To cross the raging sea
On board a man-of-war.

Some women have always taken the risk of dressing as a man and for a variety of reasons: to avoid recognition, to explore transgenderism, to obtain a man's job at a man's wage, to travel to places where it would be unsafe for a woman to travel, and to join the army or navy. Other reasons for cross-dressing are associated with gender curiosity, perhaps to enter a public house to experience a night drinking with the men, or to engage in a sexual encounter with another woman. In this era most women, with the exception of prostitutes, were banned from drinking in ale houses. For some women their personal appearance along with wearing male attire would be a public display of lesbianism. There are reports of consenting women living together, undetected for years, with some marrying and often only being discovered during the laying out process after one of them had died.

A large number of women were also starting to follow their sailor-husbands to sea during the eighteenth century, with some even openly joining their husbands on war ships. Although officially the British Admiralty did not permit women on board their vessels while at sea, many captains did in fact allow officers to have their wives on board, albeit sharing their rations, bunks or hammocks. One reason for some women to choose this harsh life was because they may have had no home or money while their husbands were at sea. The ship therefore gave them a home and the companionship of their husbands. Life was hard on board a man-of-war, with the women having little privacy and being required to stay almost hidden so as not to interact with the sailors and soldiers, who might number over 400. The women would work while on board doing tasks such as mending clothes, general maid duties and most importantly nursing sick and injured sailors and soldiers. During battles, the women assisted gun crews by carrying the gunpowder, with some being wounded or killed in action as a consequence.

Although women were commonplace on board naval ships, their presence was generally not recorded in the ships' records, largely because they were not paid for any work on board, or given their own rations by the navy. This meant that officers were not required to record the women present within the formal accounts. Officers were known to sometimes have their wives accompany them on board, but even these women failed to be mentioned in the ships' official logs. During the 1801 Egypt campaign more than 60 Royal Navy ships carried 12,000 troops to Aboukit Bay, Egypt. Surprisingly, for every 100 men three soldiers were allowed to bring their wives, and incredibly their children, on the voyage. This means that there were in the region of 360 women travelling with the fleet along with their children. For the first time these women were allowed to be fed from the ships' rations due to their being employed as invaluable nurses to tend sick and injured men. Following this initiative women started to be actively encouraged to work as nurses on board war ships. However, it should be noted that accounts at the time state that the women working on board naval ships were often sacked for prostitution, drunkenness and aiding the sailors to desert. In other words, there existed much prejudice from the authorities against women being on board a vessel once it had left port. One sailor wrote that '…those ladies are exceedingly bold and audacious…I had a great deal to do to repulse the temptations I met with from these sirens.'[129] With so many women sailing on ships it is obvious that women engaged in warfare, and would have also inevitably given birth on board ship, and also sometimes died on board. The saying "son of a gun" originates from the firing of a cannon to hasten the birth!

> This day the surgeon informed me that a woman on board had been labouring in childbirth for twelve hours, and if I could see my way to permit the firing of a broadside to leeward, nature would be assisted by the shock. I complied with the request, and she was delivered a fine male child.

So wrote Captain Glascock of the Royal Navy in his journal during the Napoleonic Wars. During 1811 Dr William Paul Crillon Barton, a young forward thinking naval surgeon, recommended that female nurses should be formally recruited as naval personnel. His proposal was ignored. Nevertheless, some serving officers saw no conflict in having women recruited into the navy, but only to perform the traditional work designated to the women. In very recent years we have seen women recruited into both the British Royal Navy and British Merchant Navy to train as engineers and deck personnel, distinct from the traditional role of nursing, and not being restricted to only serving on shore.[130]

129   Slope N. 'Women in Nelson's Navy' *BBC History*. updated 17. 02.2011. http://www. bbc.co.uk/history/british/empire_seapower/women_nelson_navy_01.shtml
130   *Women and the British Navy*. Mariners Museum. www.marinersmuseum.org

Another path that women could take to work on board a ship was to work as a stewardess, which was becoming more acceptable by the late nineteenth century. For example, Sophia Aylesbury, born in 1831, worked as a stewardess on a number of weekly ferries to Ireland. The vessels included *The Briton* (282 tons) and the *Somerset*, She earned five shillings a week during 1872. The gap between leaving Bristol and departing from either Dublin or Waterford was four days at this time. The *Somerset* was a costal trader and licensed to carry up to twelve passengers. She sailed weekly to Tenby, Wales, and is also recorded as making two voyages to Ilfracombe, Devon.[131]

Less well known is the fact that women were often responsible for the launching of lifeboats, into the ice cold seas, and then on the lifeboat's return, for hauling the boat back ashore, wading into the water, skirts tucked up. It could take up to 30 women to manually haul the boats up and down the beach with heavy, wet, harsh ropes, often in the dark and in gales. It was necessary for the women to commit to this role, not only out of compassion, but also because in smaller communities all the able men would be crewing the lifeboat. The women were of course dependent on the men as providers but at the same time the men were putting their lives at risk working as fishermen.

There are also many accounts of brave young women jumping into the high seas to save drowning sailors. Some of the heroines were daughters of lighthouse keepers and witnessed ships crashing onto nearby rocks during bad weather on the British coast. Women were also known to have bravely jumped off the end of piers to save drowning people at sea.

There were naturally women who were attracted to other women throughout history and the temptation of some transgender women would be to sometimes live life as a man in perpetuity, which was illegal, especially if committed without the knowledge of the other women involved. For example, in 1746, Mary Hamilton stood in court on a charge of 'the gross offence of marrying 14 women'. Highly unlikely, but unfortunately for Mary her self-claimed fourteenth wife gave evidence against her in court after being

---

131   During 2016 the number of female ratings in the RN stood at 9% and at 14.9% in the Maritime Volunteer Reserve. These figures have remained static since 2014. The Merchant Navy accepts women to train and serve on board ship with the total number of UK seafarers in 2016 standing at 23,060. Women in the MN account for 32% of ratings compared with only 9% active in the RN during 2014. Sources: 1. British Navy statistics obtained from the Ministry of Defence. Request for Information. Navy Command FOI Section. April. 2018. 2. U.K. Armed Forces Biannual Diversity Statics. Re-released 10 March 2016. Ministry of Defence. www.assets.publishing.service.gov.uk. 3. Merchant Navy statistics obtained from the UK Chamber of Shipping. 2018 www.assets.publishing.service.gov.uk Also Bristol Record Office.

married to her for only three months. Her punishment was read out in court by the justices:

> That the he or she prisoner at the bar is an uncommon notorious cheat, and we, the Court, do sentence her or him, whichever he or she may be, to be imprisoned for six months, and during that time to be whipped in the towns of Taunton, Glastonbury, Wells, and Shepton-Mallet.[132]

A severe penalty and a common punishment was operated by the navy to many a sailor who committed petty misdemeanours. In other words sailors, who were by nature of their occupation incarcerated on board a ship, were just as likely to find themselves being maltreated, flogged around the fleet, as the cross-dressing polygamist woman.[133] State sanctioned barbaric punishments existed on land and at sea in equal measure. Although Mary was not a sailor, her demise demonstrates the shame and confusion felt by a person desiring to cross-dress in order to feel comfortable through displaying their male gender connectedness.

When appearing in court, exposed women sailors were given an opportunity to offer testimony to explain how they came to be on board a ship, unsuspected and working as a man as part of the crew. This must have been a humiliating and fearful experience for many of these women, one that would have left them feeling subjugated before bigoted men. Some of the accounts are reported in the first person, giving us an insight into the social and working conditions for sailors at the time. It is important to be sensitive to the fact that when women were trying to offer an explanation to the men of the court, as to why they had dressed as men, they may in fact be hiding upsetting hidden truths about their personal lives. To be a transgender woman, gender curious or gender-queer at this time was considered a joke, an eccentricity, or worse still a form of insanity. Furthermore, to be a victim of childhood sexual abuse could not be mentioned, the subject was completely taboo or disbelieved. The women risked and feared not being believed; to be blamed, stigmatised, humiliated and left suffering in social disgrace. The traumatic consequences were too scandalous to bear and hence never

---

132 *Hants Telegraph.* 25 Mar. 1893.
133 1. In 1899 a letter was issued from the Admiralty that no Commanding Officer could award a sentence of more than 25 lashes. In March 1949, an Order in Council removed all authority to award corporal punishment, although the Naval Discipline Act of 1866 remained in force until 1957. *National Museum of the Royal Navy, 2014.* 2. Corporal punishment of very severe caning on bare skin was still permitted on naval training ships for boys until abolition was forced by the Labour government on a reluctant Admiralty in 1967.

to be mentioned by the women, who chose instead to make up elaborate, romanticised stories for public consumption.

The newspapers would sometimes run reports about discovered women sailors, or girl-sailor-boys, as they preferred to call the women. Usually the account would be romanticised, being common in the literary realism style of the eighteenth and nineteen centuries. The reports do not engage with the wider social and economic issues that confronted and impeded the life of women, but rather to simply offer the narrative as told in court, or to a reporter. The greater and deeper underlying social problems that caused their circumstances were not addressed by politicians until the early to mid-twentieth century. The primary premise of the reports was to be concerned with how a woman could so easily have deceived the masculine world of the sailor to such an extent that the men unknowingly, and without cause for concern, had a woman living below decks and working amongst them.

Below, in chronological order, is a sample of some of the extraordinary reports taken from the newspaper archives conveying the circumstances of women sailors who were discovered. The narratives offer a fascinating insight, not only for the evidence they present, confirming that women cross-dressed, but also, in many cases, revealing, in part at least, the reasons why these women were on a ship in the first place. Firstly, the account of a fisherwoman discovered to be working as a seadog woman out of the small fishing town of Brixham in Devon.

A Female Sailor

During July 1841, Ellen Watts, aged 16 years, and calling herself Charles Watts, was discovered to be a woman dressed in sailor clothing after being injured following a fight with a young tailor in Devon. It transpired that Ellen was protecting two young women from the tailor's unwanted advances in an orchard. Ellen had been working for some time as a fisherwoman on a trawler. After being left an orphan in Plymouth, she found herself apprenticed out (probably by the workhouse guardians) to a farmer, who forced her to work as an outdoor servant (agricultural labour). Her story continued that following her brother's drowning she dressed in her deceased brother's clothing and obtained work as a boy on board a trawling sloop as an apprentice, remaining undetected for three years. She went on to add that the reason why she had adopted life as a woman sailor 'was that she could enjoy more freedom than in domestic servitude'. In court her fellow sailors said that Ellen 'performed her duty manfully, enduring all the privations of such a precarious calling with a degree of hardihood and recklessness necessary to such a life, and her exertions were such as to cause a degree of envy in the other lads.' The report continues: 'She is now dressed in apparel more becoming her sex; she is an interesting and rather good looking girl'.[134] It is not known what became of Ellen after appearing in court, but she probably found employment as a domestic servant.

The sad story and attempted suicide of Maria Louisa Cook of Chulton, Somerset (1846)

Maria's story appeared in the *Stirling Observer* and describes how she had tried, but failed, to run away to sea as a cabin boy to follow her soldier boyfriend to Ceylon who, it was reported, had deserted her.

> On Sunday a young women dressed as a sailor boy was placed at the bar of Lambeth Police Court...on a charge of attempting to destroy herself by taking a quantity of laudanum.[135]

So wrote the London court correspondent during 1846 about Maria's appearance in court. Maria, deeply depressed, humiliated and nervous hid her face with her hands while in court; 'she concealed her face from the gaze of the crowds in court, placing her hands over it'.

Maria was apparently the daughter of a veterinary surgeon residing in the village of Chulton, Somerset. During 1843 she formed a relationship with a private in the 37th Regiment of Foot who she met in or near to Bristol. Maria explained to the magistrate that she had met the soldier three years ago when he had belonged to a recruiting party in Bristol. Some six months later she joined him in Newport, Wales, and then moved with him to Chatham. He was required to live in at Brompton Barracks, Chatham, but she had taken lodgings in the nearby town so they could still be together.

However, her lover was now to sail to Ceylon (Sri Lanka) with his regiment and, because Maria could not bear to be parted from him, in an act of desperation she came up with a plan to follow him across the world. Maria was aware that his vessel was waiting to set sail in West India Docks, in the Port of London. With this knowledge she hatched a plan to disguise herself as a cabin boy and obtain employment on his ship. Maria tells how she sold all her women's clothing "at great sacrifice", and purchased a sailor's suit. Next she made her way to the Mariners' Register Office to obtain her legal ticket to work as a "capacity boy" (cabin boy). At the office she registered herself as

---

134   The *Kerry Examiner*, 30 Jul. 1841. p.3.
135   *Stirling Observer*. 3 Dec. 1846.

a David Cook and stated she was born in Bristol on 3 August, 1830, thereby making her only sixteen years of age, although she was probably at least three years older. Unfortunately for Maria the captain already had enough hands for his sailing so she was unable to join her boyfriend on board. Now finding herself alone, friendless and destitute in London, Maria obviously fell into a deep state of depression and attempted to commit suicide by taking a quantity of laudanum in a quayside coffee house. Maria wrote a suicide letter that was read out in court to be used in evidence against her.[136]

Dear Thomas

I have overstepped the bounds of procedure and modesty, in hopes of being able to reach Ceylon with you. I have put on boy's apparel, and come to this sink of iniquity, London, to enter the *Minervea* as a boy, but when I got here the captain had shipped all his hands.

I have tried to get on board several other vessels, but cannot on account of not being able to find money enough to procure sufficient clothes to go to sea with. I have sold all my own to get what I have on, and have no money to get others. I have no friends here—no place to go—I cannot blame any person but myself. Think of me no more, Thomas, as it is useless; you will never see nor hear of me again. Remember me to Harriet and Charles. Don't make yourself at all uneasy about me. I have no more to say, but remain yours till death.

M. Cook, London. Nov. 14."

Her despairing letter to her lover is articulate and eloquently written and clearly reveals Maria to be an educated young woman. Her attempted suicide demonstrated the utter depression and lonely state that she was enduring while being forcibly separated from her boyfriend in London. Although attempting suicide was a criminal offence the magistrate seems to have taken pity on Maria as she was remanded for a week to give her time to communicate with her friends. Unfortunately we do not know what happened to her following her appearance in court, but perhaps she reluctantly returned to her family in Somerset or started a new life in London. During this time Maria would

---

136   The Suicide Act 1961 is the Act of Parliament which decriminalised the act of suicide in England and Wales. Until this time it was illegal to attempt suicide which was punishable by a prison sentence not exceeding fourteen years.

have found herself 'ruined' and with the shame of the publicity surrounding her story she would have probably changed her name and descended into obscurity.

Margaret, native of Liverpool. (1849)

Margaret was married at 17, to a man named Johnson, with whom she had an unhappy relationship, and who eventually deserted her for Canada. Her reaction was to dress as a sailor and sail as a crew member on the passenger ship *Thetis* to Newfoundland in search of her husband. Realising she would not find him there she sailed back to Liverpool on the *Thetis*. During the whole of the five months serving on board her gender was never discovered and:

> although rough weather was encountered, and she had, in course of her ordinary duties, to mount aloft, on stormy days as well as tempestuous nights, she never betrayed the slightest symptom of that fear which is supposed to attach to women only, but, on all occasions, proved herself as good a "man" as any other in the ship. After being arrested, the magistrate, Mr Rushton, signed an order for her immediate admission to the penitentiary.[137]

'Female Sailor' (1850)

> Lately, an inquest was held at the Hythe, on the body of a sailor found drowned. The jury found the usual Verdict: after-wards, when the body was stripped for burial, the supposed sailor was found to be a female—a poor girl who had been engaged in seaman's garb, only a week before, at Harwich and who had accidentally fallen over the bulwark of the vessel, at Wivenhoe.[138]

During 1859 a substantial number of stories detailing the discovery of women sailors were appearing in the press. There seems to have been a salacious public appetite for tales of cross-dressing women sailors. The Victorian melodrama was very popular at this time, both on stage and as a short story which would include villains, heroes and heroines. Many of the stories of women sailors reflected a romantic theme to the reader. Perhaps cross-dressing women were being reported in the media as the editors knew the public were curious about

137 The *Freeman's Journal*. 13 Dec. 1843.
138 *Hertford Mercury also Reformer and Essex Herald*. 8 Jul. 1850.

the theme, particularly if a court case involved a tragic account of a poor lost girl. Below follow four newspaper stories that illustrate the treatment of discovered women sailors by the media during 1859.

Annie Stewart, 1859 'The Sailor Boy Just Another Time.'

Aged just 17, Annie found herself up in court in Bristol. She had been accused of attempting to steal a dress from the property next door to her boarding house. In court, she told her story and maintained that she had worked for three years on board the *Emily Hamilton*, as a cabin boy. Recently being paid off, unsuspected of being a woman, she "could na get work" and had been robbed of her money. On hearing her story 'the Bristol Mayor raised a small subscription for her to travel to London and sail to Scotland. She left the court very pleased with the good luck that had befallen her'.[139] Being originally from Scotland, the mayor would rather that she was sent on her way so that the Bristol Corporation Guardians were not held financially responsible for her.

Annie was frequently up in court in Bristol during 1859, usually for being drunk. So notorious had Annie's disgrace become that on one occasion she found herself surrounded by a crowd after failing to leave Bristol as ordered by the court. Appearing in St Peter's Court, Gloucester Lane, on 22 November 1859, the magistrates were deciding whether or not to send her to St Peter's Asylum. (A former workhouse, but still a workhouse of sorts housing the pauper sick).[140] The court stated in the end that they would not send her back to St Peter's as "last time you were there you kept the house in a state of excitement walking up and down smoking a pipe". Instead, they sent her to prison in default of payment of a fine.

> Anne Stewart, the vagrant girl, who has several times figured at the office in the guise of a sailor boy…attired in her favourite costume, who then had a trifle given to her to help her on her way to Liverpool, was now charged with having been disorderly in Gloucester Lane. She *still* appeared in sailor's rig, but since her last appearance before the Bench had got rid of her warm jacket, so that she wore nothing above her waist but a thin shirt, and was consequently shivering from the cold…Mr. Brice said he really could not tell what it was

---

139 *Royal Cornwall Gazette*. 15 Jul. 1859.
140 St Peter's Hospital. A former workhouse for paupers, converted into a primitive workhouse hospital for the poor. By 1820, the 'hospital' had 85 pauper inmates who looked after 306 sick paupers.

best to do with her. Annie told the court "I shouldn't have been here again, but that I met a fool of a fellow on the road who promised if I would come back with him that he'd ship me...I wish you would put me in the Penitentiary, or the Reformatory, or somewhere. When I get money in my pocket I have not resolution to resist the drink. The Court "I think the best way will be to send you to a Lunatic Asylum". Annie "Onywhere, onywhere, only send me somewhere". Court "It would do you good, I think, to have your head shaved." The court was told that 'the prisoner would not wear female clothes; some ladies had tried in vain to induce her to do so.[141]

However, the very next day it was reported in the *Western Daily Press*, that:

Mr McCartney of the Caledonian Society promises to send Ann Stewart back to Scotland on release from prison, though Stewart had failed to go through with the journey previously'.

The Caledonian Society of Bristol was founded in the early nineteenth century 'for the relief of unfortunate but deserving Scotchmen'. The charity aided and provided provision of relief and benevolence, but only for those who deserved support in the opinion of the society's agents. There are many cases of interaction between the Caledonian Society and other relief agencies in Bristol recorded, as well as with the courts. If applicants for relief to the Bristol Corporation were found to be of Scottish nationality they were automatically sent to be tested by the agent of the Caledonian Society in Bristol.[142]

On the 2 December 1859, the *Western Daily Press* reported 'The Sailor Girl Nuisance'. Ann Stewart arrested drunk and disorderly at the Basin, having failed to leave Bristol again. Bound over for unwomanly conduct"... but this time she was in female attire.

Sarah Burton

Sarah Burton also found herself in Bristol Police Court during 1859, charged with being drunk the previous evening. When she was arrested she was dressed in 'male attire; and only at the police station her sex discovered'. Sarah was wearing traditional sailor's garb of a Guernsey shirt, canvas trousers, braces

---

141   *Western Daily Press*. 'The Sailor Boy Just Another Time'. 22 Nov. 1859.
142   *The Scottish Diaspora Blog*. http://www.thescottishdiaspora.net :accessed 1 May 2018.

and a blue cap, which she refused to give up, saying that she planned to sail for another three months as a seaman. Sarah had worked for a month after being paid for one month in advance. However, the captain discovered her gender before setting sail and ordered her off his vessel. The newspaper reports that 'The Bench severely lectured her on the impropriety of her conduct and discharged her'.[143]

A female sailor charged with walking about in male attire, 1859

It was dramatically reported in 1859 that 'A female sailor was awarded the protection of anonymity to prevent her being mobbed'. The anonymous woman had been charged in Newport for walking about in male attire of seaman's clothing. 'The defendant, who wore seamen clothes, in her appearance, gait, and gestures appeared to be every inch a sailor.' In court her 'quiet-looking seaman' husband, who she had married the year before, stood beside her as she told her story. For ten years she had sailed around the world undertaking heavy deck duties and loading work. 'One occasion she carried between the vessel and the shore in a day no less than 70 sacks of flour; while at the winch her courage never flagged, and her strength never failed.' Her last voyage was from Truro as an able-bodied seaman at £2.5s per month. She went on to say she had even worked as a navvy on the Exeter railway and had never been discovered to be a woman. She told how she married a year ago and worked as a ship's cook and steward to support her husband, who had met with misfortune. She was discharged.[144]

Two weeks prison, 1859

Again, in 1859 another female sailor was discovered, only her last name being recorded as Anderson, aged 17. The unfortunate woman was sentenced to two weeks imprisonment in Shepton Mallet gaol by the magistrate at Weston-Super-Mare for an act of vagrancy–sleeping in the open air for one night in a ditch near to Axbridge, Somerset. This was despite the public and former employers taking pity on her.

Here follows an abridged version of Anderson's story.

I was born at Glasgow, on 11 July, 1842. My mother died when I was three days old; my father, who was a private in the 42nd Foot regiment, married again about twenty months after the death of

---

143   *Sherbourne Mercury*. 11 Sept. 1859.
144   *Morpeth Herald*. 27 Aug. 1859.

my mother. I had four brothers all older than myself, who enlisted into the same regiment. My father being sent abroad to a foreign station. I was left at home in the care of my mother-in-law, [sic] who sent me for two years to the National School, in Argyle Street, Glasgow; at the end of that time Col. Hamilton sent me to a better school for three years. After that I worked in the printing trade, … where I worked until I was 13 years; work then becoming scarce I left. Having saved 38 shillings, I went to London and try my fortune there. I wandered about the streets for 3 or 4 days. Then one morning I saw a sailor boy pass me; and it struck me "I am as strong as he, might I not go to sea?" I went to the barbers and got my hair cut off telling him it was so heavy it made my head ache; I called at the shop of a Jew named Jacob, and bought a rig out for a sailor, selling my own clothing to him for two shillings. I worked as a cabin boy, sailing to Bristol where I was signed-off. I did not like it there in Bristol, so I tramped to Devon.[145]

The men in court took pity on her and gave her £10. The Captain appeared in court too, also contributing to her fund by giving her the £7 wages she was owed, plus another £5 about her not liking Bristol!

Thomas Stewart

Thomas Stewart, 1860, was arrested in the Royal Princess Inn, Church Street, Whitby by a constable who had heard her singing and being drunk in the street at 2am. At the time of arrest she was dressed in a Guernsey frock, a pair of tight duck trousers, with a strap about her waist and a cap. Thomas was said to have used 'filthy language to all present in the police station.' She told the magistrates on the same day that she was seventeen years of age, an orphan and originally from Glasgow. Her brothers were sailors and at the age of twelve she decided to 'follow her inclinations and go to sea also'. She went on to tell the magistrates that she had been at sea for five years, performing her duties very well, and did so to have an 'honest living'. She wanted to obtain another ship 'for a voyage of eighteen months, as she thought she should be able to save a little money, and buy herself some petticoats, and follow the calling of a female'. The Bench 'recommended the superintendent to see her safely out of the town and to give her 3s. out of the box'. On promising to leave the town without delay, she was discharged. "Tom" smokes furiously, besides indulging in quids [chewing tobacco] and nautical oaths, and her

145   *Wells Journal 20 Aug. 1859. p.4.*

appearance corroborates her statement of long sea-service. When discharged she left the court with a rolling gait.'

Thomas was soon reported drunk again that evening in Upgang, and again the next day at Hinderwell, but went on to Hartlepool to obtain a vessel.[146]

Susan Thorne

Susan Thorne, 1861 was charged with being disorderly and walking in the high street 'attired as a man-of-war's man'. It was reported that on leaving the court she shouted at the top of her voice, "old Bob Ridley, oh".[147] Susan was later mentioned in the *Western Daily Press*, 11 September 1861, being reported as a female sailor appearing in Bristol Court in sailor's clothes in High Street Market, Bristol.

The Handsome Cabin Boy

It's of a pretty female as you may understand,
Her mind being bent for the rambling into some foreign land.
She dressed herself in sailor's clothes or so it does appear,
And she hired with a captain to serve him for a year.

The captain's wife she being on board, she seemed in great joy
To think her husband had engaged such a handsome cabin boy.
And now and then she slipped him a kiss, and she would have liked to toy,
But it was the captain found out the secret of the handsome cabin boy.

Her cheeks they were like roses and her hair all in a curl,
The sailors often smiled and said, he looks just like a girl.
But eating of the captain's biscuit her colour did destroy
And the waist did swell of pretty Nell, the handsome cabin boy.

It was in the Bay of Biscay our gallant ship did plough.
One night among the sailors was a fearful flurryin' row.
They tumbled from their hammocks for their sleep it did destroy
And they swore about the groaning of the handsome cabin boy.

146   *Leeds Mercury* 19 Jan. 1860
147   *Bristol Mercury*. 11 Sept. 1861

"Oh doctor dear, oh doctor," the cabin boy did cry,
The doctor came a-running and smiling at the fun,
To think a sailor lad should have a daughter or a son.

The sailors when they saw the joke, they did stand and stare.
The child belong to none of them, they solemnly did swear.
And the captain's wife she says to him, "My dear I wish you joy,
For it's either you or I betrayed the handsome cabin boy".

So each man took his drop of rum and he drunk success to trade,
And likewise to the cabin boy who was neither man nor maid.
It's hoping the wars don't rise again, us sailors to destroy,
And here's hoping for a jolly lot more like the handsome cabin
boy.[148]

'Another Female Sailor'

In the 1850s and 60s, reports of female sailors were cropping up on a regular basis all over the country, as well as in Ireland, America and around the world; hence the editors' insertion of 'Another' into the written reports that appeared on a regular basis in the press.

Ordinary seaman William Bruce was actually Charlotte Petrie, as was dramatically reported in 1865. Her gender was discovered in the port of Palermo, Sicily, while serving on board the *Expedient*, under Captain Lane. She was found out after some of her fellow sailors saw her washing, having removed her top. But despite being discharged from her sailor life when the ship returned to London, she went on to work as a labourer for ten months at a lead works in Newcastle, alongside 150 unsuspecting men. Charlotte continued to dress in her male sailor clothes; she drank beer with the men and smoked a pipe. Her colleagues told the reporter that she would always appear at 5am to catch the daily boat to her place of work and often joined in flirting with the other young men with the young women along their way. 'On one occasion this extraordinary girl was the "spokesman" in an appeal for an increase of wages at the lead factory wherein she was in some extent successful'. How she came to be discovered is not known, but after being exposed she was so highly respected by her fellow workmen that they raised funds for a presentation for her. It was also reported that Charlotte had once again returned to her sailor career. An interesting postscript to her story is found in a defiant letter she apparently wrote to the *Man on Ross and*

148   www.mainlynorfolk.info : 'English Folk and Other Good Music'.

General Advertiser newspaper exhibiting her anger at being discharged from the *Expedient* and the patronising treatment she received from Captain Lane:

> I would take to ask Captain Lane what he did with the clothes he received from me at Palermo. He did not do his duty to me at Palermo. He did not do his duty to me when we came to London… She wishes to inform Captain Lane that she has got on without his help till now, and she can do without it yet.[149]

A Female Sailor Killed (1869)

"A female Sailor" At West Hartlepool mortuary, on Thursday the attendant, who was laying out the body of a supposed youth, discovered to be of a woman, who, under the name of Hans Brandt, had shipped as an apprentice on board the barque *Ida* of Pensacola. She was killed by a fall into the hold on Wednesday night.[150]

'The Little Deceiver'

Alice Amelia McKinley was known to her employees as 'Tommy' David James Lincoln Garfield McKinley; David, she said, being her brother's name and 'Tommy' being her nickname to the other sailors. She claimed that she was originally from Chicago and was attempting to make her way back to the city in an effort to find her mother and brother.

During the year of 1898, a sensational story reached newspaper correspondents concerning Alice McKinley who had ran away to sea in an apparent desperate effort to return to her homeland and find her family. This remarkable young woman was born in Chicago on the 22 July 1882, at 12 Clark Street and at the age of 16, she signed up as a deckhand on the S.S. *Blaenavon* setting sail from Cardiff.

Alice's original story was as follows: After the death of her father when she was 10 years old, her mother, originally from Wales, took Alice and her brother David from Chicago back to Newport, Wales, to stay with her grandmother. The mother apparently promptly deserted the children, presumably sailing back to America alone. According to records, Alice attended St. Mary's Catholic Church School in Newport for three years, until the death of her grandmother. Her brother had in the meantime gone to sea himself, running away back to America on the S.S. *Craylands* under the name

149   *Man on Ross and General Advertiser.* 14 Dec. 1865.
150   *Manchester Courier and Lancashire General Advertiser.* 14 Jun. 1890.

of James Bonici. This act was to prove pivotal to Alice's future if the story is true. Alice was next sent to live with her Maltese uncle and aunt in Newport, and at the age of 13 they placed her in domestic service at the family home of a Captain Morgan. According to Alice's account, her uncle and aunt could no longer afford to support her due to the Great Welsh Coal Strike, which would have resulted in the stoppage of shipping coal for over six months.[151] We can only surmise that Captain Morgan was in the business of transporting coal out of Newport via the sea. Research into Alice's residences while in Wales appears to indicate that she was probably bonded to Captain Morgan, and as such would have received very little pay, if any at all, with only her food and lodging provided.

Alice's account of her young life is best conveyed in her own words, through the newspaper interviews she gave at the time of her discovery. The initial interview with Alice McKinley took place while she was temporarily housed at the Scandinavian Sailors' Temperance Home, London.[152] This version of her interview is taken from the *New Zealand Herald* who published her account in full, following an interview she gave to *The Mail* (not on record) once she had returned to London. Her account of her sailing life gives a good insight of her and her sailor companions' living conditions and the type of work responsibilities a young seaman learning the profession would have to perform. The article was given the condescending title '*Interview with the Little Deceiver*' at the time of print, perhaps because the reporter felt that not all that Alice was conveying to him was the full truth:

> The plucky American girl was wearing the simple grey stuff[153] dress that was given to her at Las Palmas, and as she seated herself in readiness for the story, there was a moment in which to [gain] an impression of a small, well-rounded figure, a close-cropped head of jet black hair, a round, comely, sun-browned face, and a pair of large, dark, intelligent eyes.

151   The Welsh coal strike of 1898 was an industrial dispute involving the colliers of South Wales and Monmouthshire. The miners were attempting to remove the sliding scale rate of pay, meaning their wages were based on the price of coal. The strike led to a devastating lock out lasting six months with the miners not changing the wage system by the end of it.
152   The former Scandinavian Seamen's Temperance Hostel was located in Garford Street, near to the West Indian Docks. It was re-built in 1889 and opened by Prince Oskar of Sweden and Norway in February 1898. Originally the hostel was founded in 1880 by a Swedish Lutheran missionary Agnes Hedenström, and closed after her death in 1928. In 1930 it became a Salvation Army hostel and finally closed in June 2003. The building was sold off and is now apartments. National Maritime Museum, London.
153   A woollen dress.

To begin at the beginning', she said, 'as far as I can remember I never went to any public school, but educated myself as well as I was able. My father was a chief engineer on board an oil tank trading to this country [England]. I only remember that it was the year of the World's Fair.[154]

Her father died at sea and after this event her mother took Alice and her brother David back to her mother's country of birth:

We went to Newport, Monmouthshire, where we lived with my grandmother at 3, London Street. Soon after, my grandmother died, and we went to live with my Maltese uncle, a sea captain, who put me into service. I was 13 years of age. I was trying to save my money to give myself a little better education or to return to America. When I went back to my uncle, he said, "You had better put on your brother's suit of clothes, and go to sea." My brother, I may mention, had run away to sea some time before. I went and put on my brother's suit and went by train to Cardiff...

I wanted to go to America. None of them suspected me for I had my hair cut quite close, and looked, it seemed, just like a boy. I wanted to ship as a mess room steward if I could. One day I went to the Shipping Federation office, where I got a paper giving a description of me and my name, which I had given as David James Lincoln Garfield McKinley, my brother's name. I took the paper to all the ship owners...I finally shipped as an ordinary seaman on the British steamer *Bagnon*, Captain Thomas Enos...Took my belongings into the foc'sle. [155] There were five hands, all Welsh. Next morning we got under way for Portland. My first duty was holding cork fenders over the side. Then I was put to work cleaning

154   The World's Fair was held in Chicago in 1883 to celebrate the 400th anniversary of Christopher Columbus's arrival in the New World in 1492. Also see, *The Western Daily Press*. 31 Oct. 1898. p.5

155   The Shipping Federation was founded in 1890, in order to promote the interests of ship owners. The federation's main purpose was to oppose the increasing power of the seamens' unions and in particular the National Amalgamated Sailor's and Fireman's Union. The federation also supported free trade and strike breaking which resulted in the bankruptcy of the NASFU in 1894. However, following the sailors' and dock-workers' strike in 1911 the Federation began to recognise a place for unionisation and began to work more closely with the unions, also becoming involved in the training of seamen. The Federation began to recognise the place of unions *www.mrc-catalogue.warwick.ac.uk* .The Foc'sle is The forward part of a ship below deck, used as the crew's living quarters.

brass work. We were at sea a week and two days, and then we returned to Cardiff.

Once back at Cardiff Alice secured another job on a sailing ship, with Captain Enos sorry to see her leave. She signed on with *S.S. Blaenavon* with Captain Ferry and had been given £1 pay in advance, which Alice spent on necessaries for the voyage.

That night, at eight, I joined her [the ship] and we left about half-past nine bound for Cagliari [Italy] with a cargo of coal. There were six of us in the foc'sle, three sleeping to starboard and three to port.

At first I was terribly seasick, but I didn't mind that. They set me to work chipping steam winches. Part of my duty also was to take the 'look-out' at night on the foc'sle head, except when the hard seas were sweeping over the foc'sle. Then I went on the bridge. Everybody call me Tommy.

I knew there would be difficulties when the watch turned in, so I had to be most careful. I used to sit on a seat in the foc'sle until the men were in their bunks, and then I would turn in 'all standing', as sailors say; that is, with all my clothes on; and when the foc'sle lamp was blown out I used to undress quietly in my bunk. I don't think that for a moment I was suspected at this time.

When in port in Cagliari I noticed that some of the men had brought a girl on board. She was very young, and had her little brother with her. She came near the head of the foc'sle ladder, and a sailor brought her down below. When she got into the foc'sle a sailor pushed her over to me, saying, "Here's a sweet-heart for you Tommy". I was frightened, and said "send her out of this. For shame! Have you got no conscience". "Conscience" roared the sailors; "whd ever heard of a sailor with a conscience?" After a while the girl had something to eat and went away.

While we were in Cagliari I used to help drive the winches and look after the brass work. Just before we left I heard that we were going to Las Palmas for enough bunker coal to run us across to America, and I was overjoyed at the prospect of seeing my old home again. We left on a Monday, and next day Captain Ferry took me to the wheel

84

and told me to take hold. He said he would tell me when the ship was off her course. Before this time I had been studying a compass-card and mastering the points, so that as soon as the captain told me the course I know how the ship's head should be kept. After two or three lessons the captain said, "Why, you'll soon be able to steer like a quartermaster, my boy." From that time I took my four hours' trick at the wheel regularly, except at night, when I went for'ard on the lookout.

I never should have been found out, but for my own action. I'll tell you how it happened. One day, I think it was just before we arrived at Las Palmas. I was at the wheel. The second officer was on the bridge reading. I didn't feel up to much, and somehow something prompted me to speak. I said "Sir, you remember say on the passage out that I was more like a girl, because I cried. Well, sir, I am a girl."

The second officer put his book down slowly, and standing up facing me said "Is-that-so? You don't look much like a girl. You make a capital boy. Tonight, when you are on the look-out. I'll come for'ard and tell you whether it will be advisable to make this known to the captain or not".

That night the second officer came for'ard and said to me, "I've thought it over, and I think it will be best to tell the captain at seven bells in the morning." I was very frightened all the rest of the time, wondering what Captain Ferry would say. Just before eight bells the captain called me up on the bridge and said, with a laugh, "Here, McKinley, what's this you've been trying to stuff the men with? They say you're a girl. Is that so?" I answered as steadily as I could that it was true. He said "come into the chart-room: I want you", and then I had to go through the ignominious process of undressing. In the dreadful shame of those few moments I would… cheerfully have jumped over the side, but what could I do?…I knew Captain Ferry was a good man, and besides the chart-room door was locked. The captain was perfectly respectful, and sent me aft, telling me that for the rest of the voyage I was to help the steward, feed the chickens, and polish the brass work of the cabin door. After that I steered no more, which I very much regretted. [When the crew heard] there was a great roar of laughter in the foc'sle, and when Frenchy, one of the men, saw me, he said,

"Ah, now I know why you did not want the little girl at Cagliari for a sweetheart." Then the men would look me up and down and say "Eh, what's your girl's name? Alice eh? Well. Whatever brought you to sea? Alice?" and so on. From that time on I had my meals in the cabin with a berth to myself down aft.

The day we reached Las Palmas I was to go ashore, as the Captain was waiting for me.'

Alice rode in a buggy to the British Consul. She says the Consul and Vice-Consul were roaring in laugher which made her very angry. Alice was apparently devastated when they told her that she would not be going on to America on the *Blaenavon*,

for I was longing to see my home again and everyone in the ship had been so good to me. So I signed off the *Blaenavon*, which would have taken me to Port Kads, Mississippi where I knew there was a letter waiting for me addressed to James Garfield McKinley.

Captain Ferry shook me warmly by the hand, saying "Be a good girl", and that was the last I saw of my kind-hearted skipper.'

Alice was then taken to a Sailors' Institute where she was given a dinner, apparently much to the amusement of the Spanish maidservants who laughed at the sight of her, though she says she does not know why. The ladies bought her some women's clothing which she wore as she says for the first time in two months. Alice sailed back to London on the *Raglan Castle* and the whole ship, including the passengers, were very excited to hear about her story. She said:

[a] French lady was so excited by my experience that she repeatedly said to me "Courage! Courage!" The passengers called me Tommy, and the doctor took my photo, and everyone on board was kindness itself, for which I am very grateful…All I want now—and I want it so badly,–is to get back to America.

Alice made a visit to the United States Consulate in London, obviously trying to negotiate a passage home to New York. However, her notoriety was to follow her.

Reported in the Topeka State Journal on 22 November:

SAILOR ALICE RETURNS

Miss McKinley in America After Five Years of Adventure.

New York, Nov. 22.—One of the last passengers to land last evening from the *Paris* was a rosy-cheeked young woman clad in a tailor-made gown. A small turban hat crowned her short brown tresses and there was an anxious look in the big brown eyes as she eagerly scanned the faces of those on the pier. She was Miss Alice Amelia McKinley, but best known as "Alice the Sailor", the Chicago girl who has been roaming about the world in boy's dress for five years and most of that time doing a man's work on English transports and colliers.

Then, just two days later in the same newspaper:

MUST LEAVE AMERICA

Alice Amelia McKinley, Sailor Lassie Must Return to European Home

New York, Nov. 24—Alice Amelia McKinley, who is held by the immigration commissioners here pending an investigation into her claims of being an American, and, therefore, entitled to admission into this country, and who claims to have been born in Chicago, is beyond question an unconscionable prevaricator. She has told a half dozen different stories since her arrival on the St. Louis, three or four of which, disagreeing in every particular of detail, were spun by her today before Commissioner Mc Sweeney, the board of immigrations, newspaper reporters and others.

A correspondent saw her yesterday afternoon, and in the presence of Commissioner Mc Sweeney the girl, in answer to direct questioning, flatly confessed that she was not born in Chicago, that she had never been there, was never in the United States before and that she has no friends in the United States. She also confessed that her name was not McKinley and that she had selected it because she thought it would serve her purpose best on account of it being the name of the president. Now the girl says her name is Monroe and that she came to this country solely to get something to do "at service" because wages of domestics are higher here than in England. She also says that her father and mother are living, although a couple of hours before she had said that both were dead. The immigration officials believe her to be a natural born adventureress' [sic] brimming over with romantic inventions, as everything she has told so far has not been entitled to any credence. The pathetic tales of her adventures which have found their way into the local newspapers have failed to bring any assistance to her from charitable organizations, for the reason, no doubt, that the unreliable character of the girl romanticist is thoroughly established. Miss McKinley-Monroe will be deported.[156]

The Daily Chieftain was reporting further news about Alice by 29 December.

"Alice, sailor" A Chicago Girl who has served in the garb of a man for Five Years.

The American liner *Paris*, which arrived recently, brought from Southampton as a second-class passenger a young woman of Chicago, who is known as "Alice the Sailor". She says she has spent a number of years on the sea, all the time concealing her sex by dressing like a man. When she arrived here she was expecting to be met at the pier by representatives of the Young Women's Christian union. As none of these were present, she was taken in charge by the customs authorities.

About five years ago she left the US shipping for Cardiff, Wales, as a sailor boy. At Cardiff she went to work on a collier, and made trips to Portland, England, where she helped to coal the British warships *Repulse* and *Resolute*. Afterward she shipped on the collier *Glenavon*, and made a voyage to Caraglio, in Sardinia. During the Spanish war the *Glenavon* was chartered to take a load of coal to Las Palmas in the Canary Islands for the Spaniards. On her arrival her sex was discovered by the Spanish and they furnished her with woman's clothing and sent her to London on the steamer *Rhynland Castle*. At London she applied for help to the American consul, but as she had been away from this country for so long he would not send her home. Her story became known in London, and some

156 Ibid. Nov. 24, 1898. p.2.

of the Americans there paid her passage home—Chicago Inter Ocean.[157]

It would appear on the surface that the hopes and dreams of this abandoned young woman were to be reunited with her brother. Her story is a tragic one of motherly neglect, destitution, along with courage shown against the injustice caused by societal norms at the time. An unwilling child migrant, who first lost her father, then her mother, and finally her brother, who was searching and using her ingenuity to return to her birth home only to be rejected by her native country. Perhaps Alice was being victimised for daring to be a free-willed woman, and not knowing her womanly place, or was just an embarrassment to the authorities. Alice would have panicked being interviewed by the border agents on Ellis Island, losing her nerve, and divulged to them whatever they wanted to hear. What happened to Alice after arriving in America we simply do not know, as there appears to be no further reference to her in the newspapers.

The 1891 U.K. census does record an elderly woman, perhaps Alice's grandmother, living at 3, London Road, Newport and Alice does appear on a school register, as she stated she had attended one in an interview. In addition, a Captain Monroe, who is listed as a foreigner, appears on the census in Newport. Alice's story would appear to be partly true. But could it be that her mother had never actually been to America, and this was the part of her story that Alice was making up? We will never know the full truth. What happened to Alice after her return to London is not known, indeed even if she did return. Perhaps Alice once again disguised herself as a sailor and with her nautical experience and training she may have sailed elsewhere. It is to be doubted that Alice ever went back into domestic service; after all she had originally run away from her position in service after three years when bonded to her employer in Cardiff. It is more likely that she knew that this is what the men expected to hear her say, so she sounded compliant to their probable unsympathetic questioning in order to be released. Alice may have been a romantic fool, but she certainly had courage and determination.[158] Her story ultimately illustrates that during her seafarer's apprenticeship and experience that she was indeed a very consummate sailor.

---

157   *The Daily Chieftain*. 29 Dec.1898. p.3.

158   Alice McKinley's story was sourced from an article lodged at Auckland Libraries and APN, National Library of New Zealand. Further research has uncovered this story in more detail, thanks to an article in the *New Zealand Herald*, A Sea Romance. 'Girl ships as a sailor, how she was discovered on her second voyage.' Vol. XXXV, Is.10944, 24 Dec. 1898, p.3.

The Rambling Female Sailor. circa 1830

Come all young people far and near,
And listen to my ditty,
At Gravesend lived a maiden fair,
Who was both young and pretty.
Her lover he was press'd away,
and drowned in a foreign sea,
which caus'd this maiden to say,
This maid she was resolv'd to go
Across the foaming ocean,
She was resolv'd to let them know
How she could gain promotion.
With jacket blue and trowsers white,
Just like a sailor neat and tight
The sea it was the heart's delight
of the rambling Female Sailor . . .
From stem to stern she'd boldly go,
She brav'd all dangers, fear'd no foe,
But soon you'll hear the overthrow
Of the Rambling Female Sailor.
This maiden gay did a wager lay,
She would go aloft with any,
And up aloft she straight did go,[159]
Where times she had been many.
This maiden bold—ah, sad to tell,
She missed her hold and down she fell,
And calmly bid this world farewell!
Did the Rambling Female Sailor.
This maiden gay did fade away
Just like a drooping willow,
Which made the sailors for to say
Farewell, young faithful Willy.
When her snow-white breast in sight
became, She prov'd to be a female frame,
And Rebecca Young it was the name
Of the Rambling Female Sailor.
On the river Thames she was known full well,
Few sailors could with her excel
One tear let fall as the fate you.[160]

159 To climb the high masts, in all weathers to re-order the sails.
160 Ballad printed by W. Fordyce, Newcastle, England. www.marinersmuseu.org.

'Early Adventure of the Girl Sailor Boy' [161]

Esther McEwan was discovered wandering along Princes Street in Bristol wearing men's clothes, with 25 shillings in her pocket, by a river policeman during 1902. For this offence she was arrested and forced to appear before Bristol Police court on the 3rd of November, on a charge of 'wandering abroad without visible means of subsistence'. According to newspaper reports at the time Esther hid her face in shame and sobbed bitterly while in the dock. Apparently she was 15 or 17 years of age, depending on which newspaper report is read.

Esther had just been paid at the Board of Trade offices, for working as a mess-man and steward on board the S.S. *Gem*, which had recently docked at the Port of Bristol. The river policeman heard men discussing they had seen a woman dressed as a man wearing a rough suit of men's clothes, and he then spotted her talking to a group of sailors. When Esther was approached by the policeman she apparently burst into tears and admitted to being female, falsely telling the police officer her name was Ellen Gordon, later confessing her real name as Esther McEwan. Esther was in a rather traumatised state when she appeared in court, and was forced to tell her story in front of an all-male magistrate's court, which undoubtedly would have been a humiliating and intimidating situation.

How precisely did Esther come to be in a supposed situation of vagrancy so soon after returning to shore? According to the court reporters, before she ran away to sea Esther had been living with her married sister in rural Wishaw, Scotland. However, later accounts also suggested she was perhaps living as an orphan in Wales with her sister before she ran away to sea, but we cannot be sure which. The mystery surrounding her origins does lead us to ask a simple question: Surely her accent would have determined exactly from where in the British Isles Esther originated. Why was this not obvious to those around her when she spoke? After all, in the nineteenth century regional accents originating from Scotland and Wales were extremely broad.

It later came to light that after being orphaned (if indeed she was), Esther decided that she could make her own way in life by cutting her hair very short and dressing as a boy. As a child Esther had worked as a trolley boy at a colliery three miles from where she lived. This meant that she had adapted already to working in a majority male environment as a labourer. In fact working class teenagers and young children working as labourers, miners and factory workers were hardened from an early age to male working conditions. It would have been relatively easy for a girl to copy the mannerisms and dress code of her male co-workers. The disclosure of Esther's previous work in the

---

161   *Western Times*. 8 Nov. 1902. p.6.

mines supports the fact that the practice of exploiting children for the benefit of mine owners was still occurring at this time, despite the introduction of the 1842 Mines Act, the purpose of the Act being to supposedly outlaw all females and children less than ten years of age from working below ground. The newspaper reports do not question or ponder the fact that there were legal issues concerning her working in a mine. They report that the miners said that she 'worked in a hearty, cheery fashion, and no suspicion as to her sex was ever aroused.'[162] Esther's sister was instead blamed, 'due to ill treatment, 'her sister's harshness', 'who would make her dress as a man' to obtain work. According to Esther, after working at the colliery for four months, and on receiving her pay, she ran away to Dundee, Scotland in 1901. Esther, it would appear, was rejecting the near enslaved, abusive, labouring conditions she found herself experiencing; she took the logical decision and realised that by cross-dressing, and changing gender roles, she could improve her lot by establishing a career for herself at sea.

Esther obtained employment as a cabin boy on a coasting steamer called *Discovery*, signing on with the name of Allan Gordon after which the ship sailed to Valparaiso, Italy. On the ship's return she was discharged at Cardiff docks. She then managed to obtain another position in Penarth, Wales, and this time on board the steamer *Gem* working as a mess-room steward. The vessel sailed to Alexandria, Egypt. However, when they reached the port of Alexandria all crew had to be examined by a doctor, giving Esther no choice but to declare her sex. On her return voyage the captain had Esther travel as a cabin passenger, but by choice she remained in men's clothing until her arrest in Bristol.

The *Western Chronicle* reported that the girl was 'quick witted and had a fair education and that the rough manner of sailors on the ships in which she sailed were very repellent to her'. She told the court that "she did not like the sea at all, and had she only known the way in which she would have had to rough it would never have run away." It was also reported 'The girl is now receiving kindly care and attention'[163]...'buxom-sonsie-looking, fair hair cut short'.[164] 'In the meantime she was being looked after by the court-keepers wife', according to reports in the *Evening News*.[165] The following week *The Evening News* declared: 'The Girl Sailor—Esther McEwan, the girl sailor whose sea adventures excited such widespread interest, is now settled in a situation in Bristol as a domestic servant.'[166]

162 Ibid. 8 Nov.1902. p.6.
163 *Western Chronicle.*7 Nov. 1902. p.8.
164 Sonsie (or sonsy): A Scottish word meaning to have an attractive and healthy appearance.
165 *Evening News* 6 Nov. 1902.
166 Ibid. 13 Nov. 1902.

On 11 November, 1902, just a week after her remand, the *Bideford Weekly Gazette* reported that the girl, Esther McEwan, 'was now in female costume' and that 'a sister in South Wales has communicated with the British police', and was travelling to Bristol. In the meantime 'arrangements were being made for the girl to enter domestic service'. Girls and young women in Esther's displaced pauper situation would often be 'put out' into domestic service as a means to keep them off the parish, i.e. avoiding the rate payer and the workhouses having to provide for them. Undoubtedly Esther was far better off working as a domestic than having to reside in one of Bristol's disease ridden workhouses. Esther had probably told the court that she was from Scotland so that she might secure a passage there, paid for by the parish. Perhaps by changing her story from that of a Welsh orphan, Esther was trying to avoid the authorities sending her back to her sister's parish in Wales; after all, by Esther's own account she was a victim of abuse.

There were many unanswered questions that were not apparently of concern to the Court or to society in Bristol about Esther's circumstances. The newspaper records do not tell us any more of her story. Furthermore, there is no record of a female of her name in the 1911 Bristol census records, perhaps because Esther may have married by this time or moved on. However, extensive research of the census records shows only one person by the name of Esther McEwan recorded in the 1891 census, aged 10 years. This girl resided next door to her cousin, named Allan Gordon, an apprentice in the shipyards, the same alias that Esther gave to her employers. The girl's father was recorded as being a shipwright and the family lived in Humber, a large sailortown on the east coast of England. If she is the Esther who ran away to sea, the census indicates that her age was in fact 20 in 1901 and not 15 as reported in the court. It would also explain the lack of a Scottish or Welsh accent. Although we do not know why Esther had run away to sea, we can surmise that the unfair attitudes that restricted women's lives during this time sometimes drove some women to drastic lengths. In Esther's case it might be that she had committed a crime of some sort, was the victim of a crime, or found herself pregnant and was forced to leave home. Another possibility is perhaps undisclosed and unpleasant childhood experiences that she could not explain to a male only court or policeman. She had therefore made up her story and was hoping that the authorities would take pity on her. It appears that Esther was an enigma, and was in disguise in more ways than one.

The accounts of hard working women who served on board ships seemed to be judged as out of the ordinary. The anonymous sailor woman of 1859, while in court in Newport, talked of how she carried 70 sacks onto the dock in one day. However, carrying heavy loads was common in the work place for

Fisherwomen, Cullercoats by Winslow Homer, 1881.

working class women. Women of sailortowns and fishing ports would carry heavy baskets of fish, heavy nets and fish pots, dig for bait, and drag heavy timber fishing boats and lifeboats onto the shore. This was the prescribed traditional female 'outside' shoreline employment until many women from the coast were forced for economic reasons to migrate into the towns. An example of women carrying heavy goods is to be found in 1807 when a 'whole army' of 30,000 women were employed in seasonal employment, carrying fruit and vegetables from market gardens to the London markets twice a day.[167]

The stories that appeared in the newspapers were typically romanticised to appeal to the sentiments of the middle-class Victorian reader; inevitably with an element of grief, loss of love, abandonment and a reinforcement of patriarchal middle-class attitudes towards the foolishness of working class women. Although in fairness the newspapers, just as today, were appealing to the salacious appetites of their readers' astonishment on the discovery of cross-dressing women, living undetected with men. The discovered women would sometimes be taken pity on by their observers, and other times mocked and disciplined by the magistrates. To some the womanly deception was considered a harmless act–a girlish prank. While to others their womanly fearlessness and self-assurance seemed to threaten the construct and norms of

167   Linebaugh, op. cit. p.144.

Georgian and Victorian society. The prerequisite to maintain a strict divide of the sexes was of a godly nature of natural order, and anything else was considered unnatural. Vagrancy, due to unemployment, enclosures (forced evictions off the land), and homelessness was deeply frowned upon and caused many families to end up on the parish, something the authorities were eager to avoid. The issuing of (re)settlement orders in order to return vagrants/destitute persons back to their parish of birth, where possible, was common practice for the women of sailortown.

A very touching end was given to a drowned female sailor known only as Billy in the *Illustrated Police News* during 1873. There is indeed held within this statement a complete and absolute respect shown for the woman, but also at the same time it was considered that Billy must have had 'a strange thirst' to want to be a sailor because she was female.

'Atlantic Tragedy'

One of the stranger incidents connected with an Atlantic tragedy was the discovery that one of the bodies, apparently that of a common sailor, on the ship's crew, was that of a young woman some twenty years of age. Her sex was not found out until preparations were being made for her burial. "Billy", the name by which she was known among the crew of the ship, was a good fellow and a general favourite, taking her grog and tobacco with the roughest of them, although superior to her companions in deportment. Whatever the life of the poor girl may have been, her death was that of a self-sacrificing heroine, for she perished in attempting to save others, when many of her companions were intent on self-preservation only. Her secret, whatever it may have been, whether of unhappy love, or unrequited passion, or bitter remorse, or a strange thirst for the perilous adventures of the ocean, perished with her in the rude waves, which have swallowed up in their bosoms so many of the sorrows and mysteries of life.[168]

168   *Illustrated Police News*. 3 May 1873.

Conclusion

How many women ran away to sea is not known, as only those that were discovered and recorded are in the sources. However, the evidence does reveal that women took this action for a variety of reasons. They were all radical in their own way, but for most there certainly existed an act of rebellion and for others an act of desperation. These women were breaking and challenging social norms, and their narratives demonstrate that some were mavericks while others felt rejected and abandoned by society. For a variety of reasons the women decided to make their own way in the world and took advantage of the higher wages paid to men. It is plausible, just as today, that the women were seeking adventure and enjoyed life as a seafarer, which certainly opened up a new world to them. Although they undoubtedly experienced the same dangers that men endured sailing the high seas, the women all had one thing in common, and that was that they did not like what life had to offer them on the land. Sailing gave the women a sense of freedom and free passage to other lands for those escaping from unhappy circumstances in their sailortowns. It could be argued that these seadog women were carrying out an early initiative of equal pay for equal work. Indeed testimonies from their peers demonstrate that these women proved they could do the difficult, heavy and the dangerous work of a male sailor.

The history of women at sea and living on the margins of the sea, in sailortowns or in fishing villages is a long and varied one. The sexes had been polarised throughout early modern and modern history and none so much so as in the closed, conservative and fiercely masculine world of seafarers. Women were subjected in a systemic patriarchal inequitable society that acted as a force to suppress a female vision of the world. The evidence suggests that this sense of a 'gender segregated world order', under the judgement of the authorities of the day, in our case the Admiralty, merchant ship owners and the courts, offered no compromise. However, a paradox existed. When women sailors were discovered, it appears that their male sailor comrades would support the welfare of the women until they reached port and later state in court that the women worked hard on board ship. The 'togetherness' below decks suggests to us that the women were accepted as part of a proletarian 'collective' in the sailor fraternity. After all, the women worked hard and could be just as much victims of the harshness of naval and seafaring life as the men.

The land increasingly became mechanised with the coming of the Industrial Revolution. The development of industrial capitalism in the nineteenth century in Britain led to the engagement of women and children in the new factories and even in the mines. For these women their lives were forged by the near social disaster of the Industrial Revolution–the human cost of mechanisation. It had become the norm for the working class to be denied any rights under the governments of the time. Exploitation and suffering to produce great wealth for the few had fuelled a new class of merchants and landowners; the bourgeoisie who had developed from the slave-owning mercantilists of the eighteenth century. This resulted in a new poor urban working class, whilst at the same time hundreds of thousands of enslaved African women, men and children laboured on Caribbean plantations, fuelling the Industrial Revolution.

Meanwhile, the displaced rural labourers of Britain were rapidly moving into poorly built and cramped new towns, causing infant mortality rates to soar and a proliferation of contagious diseases. Wages were suppressed, and this trapped many women into servitude and low paid work. In an era when women had few or no rights, some women, desiring independence, saw an opportunity to escape a life that was simply not for them, that of low waged domestic servitude, perhaps a dead end exploitative factory job, or the inevitable high-risk inconvenience of bearing too many children.

Black women sailors and soldiers offer an even more remarkable story. They risked far more. This was their chance to be free people in European society, to be released from enslavement in the plantations, domestic servitude or worse. The stakes were even higher for black women working on ships that plied the triangular trade: not only because these voyages were so dangerous, but also because they were vulnerable to re-enslavement if discovered. However, as we see in Phillips's journal, all crew, regardless of colour, seemed to be treated equally as badly.

When discovered, women sailors were made to appear in court on charges of vagrancy and masquerading in male attire, effectively cross-dressing. Remarkably, it would appear that an element of compassion was expressed on the part of the men in judgement towards the women's predicament. The problem was subsequently that the women were now unable to return to their independent means of living on board ship and that they had therefore lost their home, rations and salary. At other times a good fatherly telling off was dispensed to the humiliated women, and even the poorhouse or prison might be the outcome if they could not support themselves. Women then, just as now, had to find the courage to tell the truth and to face the humiliation of not being believed in court. As a consequence, just as today, many women decided to keep their often tragic stories hidden, in fear of being dismissed as hysterical. They rightly believed they would not be understood by a system that was historically patriarchal and dominated by an elite class of men who led narrow lives.

Transvestism, gender curiosity and cross-dressing is characteristic of life for some women who feel drawn to the world of men, and for some of our women sailors who wanted to work and live as a male. Therefore, it was only natural that the male seafaring life was a draw to the gender curious woman. Some women sailors, who probably considered their sex to be male rather than female, and being gender dysphoric, found dressing in military uniform a compromise to satisfy their life-style circumstance. Fascinatingly many male seamen and colleagues completely accepted their gender switch on being discovered, even recording their respect for the women's nautical achievements. For other women the wearing of male clothing would continue, for the remainder of their lives, simply because this was the gender they choose to live.[169] Women would have been familiar with cross-dressing women and men. Female actors commonly dressed up as men on stage, which was very fashionable at the time in the many small music halls located in sailortowns, offering cheap entertainment to the working classes. Hannah Snell continued to wear her naval uniform after leaving the navy to undertake a successful music hall tour, where she would sing and march up and down the stage recounting her life as a sailor.

Women who worked as prostitutes may not have seen much difference from selling their labour in the unregulated Victorian market to that of selling their labour for human company, and at times sexual favours. Certainly for some women prostitution would simply prove to be another form of exploitation, but for others a means to live an independent life, and for some eventually marrying their sailor lovers. During 1867 over 300 prostitutes marched to the Grand Parade in Portsmouth to protest about the closure of the dockside brothels in the port city.[170] Prostitution was an easy target during an era of moral crusade with the Admiralty blaming the women for the spread of sexual diseases instead of attributing to sailors the carrying of and spreading disease. Ironically, these women were victims of their own success, and naturally by closing the brothels their work places became secret and hidden, leaving women vulnerable to violent attack and rape.

Nautical women were always the support network for sailors both on the land and in sailortowns. Women often opposed impressment and would openly attack members of the press gang, pleading for the release of their men. This was a form of political protest at a time when women had no formal

169   A later example can be found with Mary Sophia Allen (1878-1964), a former suffragette, commandant of the Women Police Volunteers, and member of the British Union of Fascists. Mary, a lesbian, continued to wear her woman's police uniform for the rest of her life. See Caldicott R. op. cit.

170   Sykes T. *Riot, Revolt and Rebellion: A Portsmouth Timeline.* www.starandcrescent.org. uk 16 Feb. 2015. accessed 19 May 2018.

political power, but could and would involve themselves in riots and protest. Some women were also deeply involved in the abolition movement, holding meetings, writing poetry and pamphlets, setting out why they felt slavery must be abolished. The abolition movement was one of the few political causes that women were able to lead and openly engage in, with women also being active in the early trade union movement.

Worth a mention are the many thousands of women who had to flee on ships in times of pogroms, famine and war. There are many stories of women, sometimes pregnant, fleeing poverty from Eastern Europe by dressing up as men to gain a passage on board the same ship as their husbands. Harshly, ships with free sponsored berths would only allow men to immigrate as the first person to be re-settled in the United States of America, with their families to follow. The U.S. census brings to light a typical example of why a woman would dress as a man to go to sea. Katherina Heintz was born at sea on May 1, 1884 because her mother Christina smuggled herself on board the S.S. *Werra* dressed as a man so she could accompany her husband to the United States and take advantage of a free sailing passage. The Heintz family were German-Russian immigrants from the southern Germanic colony in Neu Freudental, Crimea, Russia. The father, Henry Heintz, took advantage of a passage paid for by the Lutheran Church, a neo–colonial policy founded on a strategy to re-populate the mid-west of America with white, Christian, experienced farming families. On arrival they were granted free housing along with a plot of fertile Pierre land, in this case situated in North Dakota.[171] Other family members would be expected to follow the men once they had established themselves. This is an example of women, although not directly considered as nautical women, nevertheless forced to go to sea as passengers disguised as men as a means to be transported to a new life.

A few women by the late nineteenth century were allowed to work on ships as salaried nurses and stewardesses, although these women were usually in some way related to the captain or first mate. The women were a welcome hand on board ship and would have learnt new skills and gained confidence, making them stronger when they arrived home in sailortown. Despite their subordination, all the women mentioned herein were pioneers and heroines. They were courageous in their own way and unknowingly led a very slow path culminating in women eventually becoming accepted into a new navy of women: the 7,000 pioneers of the Women's Royal Naval Service–the WRENS.

The WRENS were formed in 1917. The women were able to work in a shore-based capacity as nurses, cooks, stewards, dispatch riders, sail makers

171   For a fascinating history of German migration to Southern Russia, visit Wiseman R E. 1996. *Neu Freudental—1848 Village History.* www.grhs.org/vr/vhistory/neu_freudental.htm

and in intelligence. The WRENS motto was surprisingly 'Never at Sea'. It was not until 1990 that women were actually able to serve on ships at sea. Three years later the WRENS were disbanded and women are now fully assimilated into the Royal Navy. Today women are able to serve in the Navy as both ratings, and officers. The Armed Forces had exemption from the 2010 Equality Act, for reasons of 'combat effectiveness', and up until recently there were still restrictions on females serving in close-combat roles. The ban on women crew serving on board submarines was finally ended in 2011, followed in 2018 by the lifting of all restrictions on frontline combat roles. Women can now serve in the elite forces such as the S.A.S. and the Royal Marines. The Royal Navy declares that their ethos 'is that of diversity and inclusion; this is why Royal Navy jobs are open to everyone regardless of sex, race, religion, sexual orientation or gender….We are resolutely committed to ensuring that all Naval Service personnel shall have equality of opportunity for employment—noting that minimum exemptions from discrimination law are endorsed in order to safeguard operational effectiveness'.[172] However, women still have to overcome the restrictions imposed by mandatory equipment being too heavy for them to handle and are required to wear equipment originally designed for the male frame. For example, female crew complain that the smoke hoods and breathing apparatus, required to be worn during fire drills, and in action, are unreasonably heavy for them to wear for prolonged periods. Just as in the past ships have traditionally been designed by men, for men, and thereby the measured physical strength and needs of men.

Despite these shortcomings, nautical women have come a long way since the women of sailortowns were excluded from openly going to sea, with their contribution in the nautical sphere ignored despite thousands of women actively contributing to naval operations, the transportation of cargo and in the lifeboat service.

Today women volunteer in launching lifeboats off the coast of Britain. They are known as Shore Crew with most being based in the south east.[173] In 1969 the first woman was able to work officially for the Royal National Lifeboat Institution (RNLI). Her name is Elizabeth Hostvedt, a Norwegian student who qualified at the age of 18 years to command an inshore lifeboat. To begin with, Elizabeth's request to train and join the crew of the RNLI Atlantic College Lifeboat Station was met with resistance from the authorities. Men had doubts over whether a woman would have the strength to pull heavy bodies from the water, and to crew a lifeboat in strong gales.[174] The women

---

172 *Equality, Diversity and Inclusion.* www.royalnavy.mod.uk accessed May 2018.
173 Hennessy S. *Hidden Depths. Women of the RNLI.* The History Press. 2010.
174 www.rnli.org>ourhistory>timeline 1969: First trained woman on the crew–RNLI

who have now passed the medical and arduous service tests for the RNLI have proved that women in the past would have been able to withstand the hard physical work required on former sailing vessels and to save people from the water.

Women are now accepted on ships, working alongside male sailors and sharing a collective space. In the strictly regulated hierarchical world of seafaring, this is an achievement for both women and men alike.

Homeward Bound

Though the sunshine of the tropics, around the bleak and dreary horn,
Half across the little planet lies our way,
We shall leave the land behind us like a welcome that's outworn
When we see the reeling mastheads swing and away.
Through the weather fair or stormy, in the clam and in the gale,
We shall heave behind and haul to help her, we shall hold her on her track,
And you'll hear the chorus rolling when the hands are making sail.
For the girls have got the tow-rope, an' they're hauling in the slack!

—D.H. Rogers (Date unknown)

THE END

References

Books

Baldwin, Cradock & Joy. *The London Register or a View of the History, Politics, and Literature, for the year 1815.* London. 1824.

Ball R. Parkin D. & Mills S. *100 Fishponds Rd. Life and Death in a Victorian Workhouse.* Bristol Radical History Group. Pamphleteer #34. 2015.

Bentham M.S. *The Life of Brigadier-General Sir Samuel Bentham.* Longman 1862.

Bolster W. J. *Black Jacks: African American Seamen in the Age of Sail.* Harvard University Press. 1997.

Burton V.' The work and home life of seafarers, with special reference to the port of Southampton', 1870-1921. *London School of Economics. PhD theses.* 1988.

Caldicott R.L. *Lady Blackshirts. The Perils of Perception – suffragettes who became fascists.* Bristol Radical History Group. Pamphleteer. #39. 2017.

Caldicott R. L. *The Life and Death of Hannah Wiltshire: A Case Study of Bedminster Union Workhouse and Victorian Social Attitudes on Epilepsy.* Bristol Radical Pamphleteer #35, 2nd rev. 2016.

Caldicott R.L. In Duffus J. *The Women Who Built Bristol.* Tangent Books. 2018.

Coats, A.V. *The Naval Mutinies of 1797: Unity and Perseverance.* Boydell Press: Suffolk. 2001.

Cordingly D. *Heroines & Harlots. Women at Sea in the Great age of Sail.* Macmillan. 2000.

Cordingly D. *Women Sailors & Sailors' Women.* Random House. 2001.

Disraeli B. *Sybil, Or the Two Nations.* Oxford University Press. 1998.

Dresser M. *Slavery Obscured. The Social History of the Slave Trade in an English Provincial Port.* Continuum. 2001.

Dresser M. *Slavery Obscured. The Social History of the Slave Trade in Bristol.* Bristol: Redcliffe Press Ltd. 2007.

Duffus J. *The Women Who Built Bristol.* Tangent Books. 2018.

Floud R. et al. *Height, health and history: Nutritional status in the United Kingdom 1750-1980.* Cambridge University Press. 1990.

Fryer P. *Staying Power: The History of Black People in Britain.* London. 1984.

Hair, H. & Law R. *The English in Western Africa to 1700.* Nicholas Canny, ed., *The Origins of Empire: British Overseas Enterprise to the Close of the Seventeenth Century, The Oxford History of the British Empire,* Vol. 1, Oxford: Oxford University Press. 1998.

Hennessy, S. *Hidden Depths. Women of the RNLI.* The History Press. 2010.

Hochschild, A. *Bury the Chains. The British Struggle to Abolish Slavery.* Houghton Mifflin and Co. 2005.

Hunt William. *Bristol.* London. 1895.

Land I. *Domesticating the Empire: Culture, Masculinity and Empire in Britain, 1770-1820'* PhD. dissertation University of Michigan. 1999.

Linebaugh P. *The London Hanged. Crime and Civil Society by the Eighteenth Century*. London: Verso, 2006.

Linebaugh P. and Rediker M. *The Many-Headed Hydra. Sailors, Slaves, Commoners, and the Hidden History of the Revolutionary Atlantic*. Beacon Press, Boston. 2000.

Norton R. ed. *Homosexuality in Eighteenth-Century England: A Sourcebook*. Updated 27 Feb. 2018. http://rictornorton.co.uk/eighteen

Olusoga, D. *Black and British: A Forgotten History* London: Pan, 2017.

Poole S. ed. *A City Built Upon the Water. Maritime Bristol 1750-1900*. Bristol: Redcliffe Press, 2013.

Pool, S. and Rogers, N. *Bristol from Below. Law, Authority and Protest in a Georgian City*. The Boydell Press. 2017

Powell J. 'Press Gang Violently Thwarted at Blakeney'. *Forest of Dean Local History Society*. Aug. 2017.

Richardson, M. *Pirates to Proletarians. The Experience of the Pilots and Watermen of Crockerne Pill in the Nineteenth Century*. Bristol Radical Pamphleteer #23. 2012

Rediker, M. *Between the Devil and the Deep Blue Sea. Merchant Seamen, Pirates and the Anglo-American Maritime World, 1700-1750*. Cambridge University Press. 1989.

Rogers, N. The *Press Gang. Naval Impressment and its opponents in Georgian Britain*. Bloomsbury. 2009.

Spavens W. 1796. Ed. N.A.M Rodger. *Memoirs of a Seafaring Life. The Narrative of William Spavens. Pensioner on the Navel Chest at Chatham*. The Bath Press, Bath. For the members of The Folio Society, MM. 2000.

Stark S. J. *Female Tars. Women aboard ship in the Age of Sail*. Pimlico. 1998.

Steeds M. *Cry Freedom, Cry Seven Stars. Thomas Clarkson In Bristol, 1787*. Bristol Radical Pamphleteer #1. 2012.

Stephen. L. ed. *Dictionary of Biography: Volumes 1-120*. Oxford University Press 1921-1922. vol.22 p.15.

Stokes S. 1806-1807 and 1809-1815: 'His Life in the Merchant and Royal Navies'. Unpublished journal.

Wollstonecraft M. '*A Vindication of the Rights of Woman*'. First published in1883. Dover Pub. Inc. 1996.

Wright R.J.B. '*The Royal Dockyards in England at the time of the American War of Independence*'. PhD dissertation. London University. 1972.

Journals

Baldwin, Cradock, and Joy. *The London Register or a View of the History, Politics, and Literature, for the year 1815*. London. 1824.

Beaven B. The resilience of sailortown culture in English navel ports, c.1820-1900. *Urban History*, 43, 1. 2016. p.79.

Behrendt S.D., Hurley R.A. Liverpool as a trading port: Sailors' residences, African migrants, occupational change and probated wealth. *International Journal of Maritime History*. Vol. 29 issue 4. pp: 875-910.

Carlos A.M. and Kruse J. B. 'The Decline of the Royal African Company'

Economic History Review 49, no.2. 1996.

Eltis D. 'The Volume and African Origins of the British Slave Trade before 1714'. *Cahiers d'etudes Africain*. vol. 35, no.138-139.

Foy C. R. 'The Royal Navy's employment of black mariners and maritime workers, 1754-1783'. *The International Journal of Maritime History*. 2016. Vol. 28 no. pp.6-35.

Lindert P. 1994. '*Unequal living standards*'. *The economic history of Britain since 1700*. Vol.1:357. p.86. Cambridge University Press.

Magra C. 2013. Anti-Impressment Riots and the Origins of the Age of Revolution, Mutiny and Maritime Radicalism in the Age of Revolution: A Global Survey. *International Review of Social History*. Special Issue 21. pp. 131-151.

Murdoch S. 'John Brown: A Black Female Soldier in the Royal African Company' *World History Connected*. Vol.1, is.2.

Phillips T. 1732. *A Journal of a Voyage made in the Hannibal of London, Ann. 1693, 1694, From England to Cape Monseradoe, in Africa, and thence along the Coast of Guiney to Whidaw, the Island of St. Thomas, and so forward to Barbadoes. With a Cursory Account of the Country, the People, their Manners, Forts, Trade, etc*. p.3. Published by Churchill 1732, within a *Collection of Voyages and Travels. Vol.I.* http://play.google.com/books

Rupprecht A. "Inherent Vice": Marine Insurance, Slave Ship Rebellion and the Law." *Race & Class*. Jan 18, 2018. p.6. Sage Journals. http://doi.org/10.117/0306396815611849

Unpublished journal. '*Samuel Stokes, 1806-1807 and 1809-1815: His Life in the Merchant and Royal Navies.*'

Film

Made in Dagenham. Director Nigel Cole. Paramount Pictures. 2010.

Music

The Murder City Devils. Press Gang. (Released 2000). *In Name and Blood* track list, also on live album R.I.P 2003. Worth a listen of live recording on www.youtube.com

www.mainlynorfolk.info : 'English Folk and Other Good Music'.

Fordyce W. Newcastle, England. Ballard printers.

Blogs and websites.

Ball R. 'Edward Colston Research Paper #1. Calculating the number of enslaved Africans transported by the Royal African Company during Edward Colston's involvement (1680-92).' *Bristol Radical History Group*. 2017. www.brh.org.uk

Barry, J. *College of Medicine & Veterinary Medicine. The University of Edinburgh*. 2018. https://www.ed.ac.uk/medicine-vet-medicine/about/history/women/james-barry

Caldicott, R. L. '*Should society memorialise a Slave Trader? The curious story of Brecon Town Council and the Plaque in honour of Captain Thomas Phillips, Slave Trader. (circa 1664-1713).*' Bristol Radical History. 2018. https://www.brh.org.uk/site/articles/

Costello, R. *Liverpool Black Community: The Early Years* Black History 365 Accessed 2018: https://www.blackhistorymonth.org.uk/article/section/real-stories/liverpool-black-community-early-years/

Evan J. Gloucestershire Crime History. *Masquerading as a Man: A Gloucestershire servant arrested in London, 1913.* www.gloscrimehistory.wordpress.com Published 28 Mar. 2018.

A Family History Story. http://www.afamilystory.co.uk/history/wages-and-prices.aspx#Weekly-budget

Find My Past *Britain, Royal African Company 1694-1743* https://search.findmypast.co.uk/search-world-Records/britain-royal-african-company-1694-1743-browse

'*Jack Tar: Myth and Reality' More than a List of Crew.* Memorial University of Newfoundland. 2011. www.mun.ca

Harris B. "Slaves of the Needle" The Seamstress in the 1840's. *The Victorian Web* www.victorianweb.org

Land I. *Nauticus Philo "A proposal for the encouragement of seamen"* in Bromley, ed. 2015. As cited in *Port Towns & Urban Cultures.* Pub.3 Aug 2015. www.porttowns.port.ac.uk

Major. J. *Hannah Snell: The Amazons and the Press Gang, 1771.* All Things Georgian. www.georgianera.wordpress.com

Paul J.H. '*The maintenance of British slaving forts in Africa: the activities of joint-stock companies and the Royal Navy'.* http://www.unav.edu/documents.

Slope N. 'Women in Nelson's Navy' *BBC History.* Updated 17. 02.2011. http://www.bbc.co.uk/history/british/empire_seapower/women_nelson_navy_01.shtml

Sykes T. *Riot, Revolt and Rebellion: A Portsmouth Timeline.* www.starandcrescent.org.uk Published 16 Feb. 2015.

Ward Edward (Ned). *The London-spy; and vanities and vices of the town exposed to View (1667-1731).* George H Doran Company, New York. (n.k.). University of Michigan. www.babel.hathitrust.org

Wiseman R E. 1996. *Neu Freudental – 1848 Village History.* www.grhs.org/vr/vhistory/neu_freudental.htm

Wojtczak H. British Women's Emancipation since the Renaissance: A Central Resource of Information and Primary Sources. 2009. www.http://historyofwomen.org

www.mli.org>ourhistory>timeline 1969: First trained woman on the crew – RNLI

Newspapers

Bristol Mercury. 9 Dec. 1890.
Bristol Mercury and Daily Post. 10 Mar. 1818
Bristol Post. 15 Nov. 2016
Evening News. 6 Nov. 1902.
Hants Telegraph. 25 Mar. 1893.
Hertford Mercury also Reformer and Essex Herald. 8 Jul. 1850.
Illustrated Police News. 1873.
Leeds Mercury. 19 Jan. 1860.
Man on Ross and General Advertiser. 14 Dec. 1865.
Manchester Courier and Lancashire General Advertiser. 14 Jun. 1890.
Morpeth Herald. 27 Aug. 1859.
New Zealand Herald, 'A Sea Romance. Girl ships as a sailor, how she was discovered on her second voyage.' Vol. XXXV, Is.10944, 24 Dec.1898 p.3. National Library of New Zealand.
Stirling Observer. 3 Dec. 1846.
Royal Cornwall Gazette. 15 Jul. 1859.
Sherbourne Mercury. 11 Sept. 1855.
The Freeman's Journal. 13 Dec. 1843.
Wells Journal 20 Aug. 1859
*Western Chronicle.*7 Nov. 1902.
The Western Daily Press. 31 Oct. 1898.
Western Daily Times. 1 Dec. 1849. 'A Thrilling Narrative' (From the Reports of "Labour and the Poor", in *The Morning Chronicle).*
Western Times. 8 Nov. 1892.

Suggested further reading

Steeds M. *Cry Freedom, Cry Seven Stars. Thomas Clarkson In Bristol, 1787.* Bristol Radical Pamphleteer #1. 2012. Observations of abolitionist Thomas Clarkson while in Bristol researching the conditions for crew on board slave ships.

For a thorough and comprehensive list of examples and newspaper articles on cross-dressing women from all sections of society see: Rictor Norton (Ed.). *Homosexuality in Eighteenth-Century England: A Sourcebook.* Available at http://rictornorton.co.uk

For the history of Bristol's pilots and their struggle to defend their jobs and traditions and eventual involvement in the wider labour movement see Mike Richardson *Pirates to Proletarian. The Experience of the Pilots and Waterman of Crockerne Pill in the Nineteenth Century.* Bristol Radical Pamphleteer. Pamphlet #23. 2012.

A comprehensive and wonderfully illustrated book on the history of the involvement of women in the Royal National Lifeboat Institution (RNLI) can be found in Sue Hennessy *Hidden Depths. Women of the RNLI.* The History Press. 2010.